Stillbirth, Yet Still Born

Grieving and Honoring Your Precious Baby

Deborah L. Davis, PhD
Author of *Empty Cradle, Broken Heart*

FULCRUM

Library of Congress Cataloging-in-Publication Data

Davis, Deborah L., 1955-
  Stillbirth, yet still born : grieving and honoring your precious baby / Deborah L. Davis.
    pages cm
  Summary: "This small book offers tailored information and support to accompany parents through the early hours, days, and weeks that follow the death and birth of their beloved baby. It also offers strategies for enduring labor and delivery, and compassionate suggestions for spending time with the little one. Parents will find ideas for affirming and honoring their precious baby's life"-- Provided by publisher.
  ISBN 978-1-938486-33-3 (paperback)
1. Perinatal death--Psychological aspects. 2. Stillbirth--Psychological aspects. 3. Infants--Death--Psychological aspects. 4. Parents--Psychology. I. Title.
  RG631.D39 2014
  618.3'92--dc23

                    2014015083

Printed in the United States of America
0 9 8 7 6 5 4 3 2 1

Designed by Ken Lockwood

Fulcrum Publishing
4690 Table Mountain Dr., Ste. 100
Golden, CO 80403
800-992-2908 • 303-277-1623
www.fulcrumbooks.com

This book is dedicated to the parents
who contributed to this book;
to their babies;
to your babies.

In loving memory . . .

Helen Alice Anderson
Carrie Jean Beck
Mia Donegan Buri and Grace Donegan Buri
Stetson Alan Carroll
Morgan Nicole Dahl
Sasha Felix Daly
Gabriel Overend Fortmeyer
Nathan Thomas Genser
Dominick Davis Gustafson
Emmerson Joy Hauschildt
Thor Ehrstine Heineman
Andrew Robert Hill
James Avery Hoskyn
Sarah Elizabeth Johnson
Bryce Neily Martini
Kayla Mae McFarland
Emily Anne Morrison
Oren Jasper Knight Mudrick
David Danielson Nelson
D.J. Nordlund
Kayley Amanda Oak
Rachael Louise Pozza

Laure Pryce
Jacob Walter Ramsperger
Robert Evan Reed
Adam John Ridler
Jenna Louise Robertson
Andrew James Roehl
Grace Elizabeth Roering
Lauren Nicole Schaper
Joshua David Schneider
Finley John Scott
Matthew Talaski
Tiffany Talaski
Pierce Robert VanDerMeer
Joseph David Wilson
Olivia Catherine Wittman
Sarah Rose Yellovich
Lynn Zimmer

Contents

World Turned Upside Down

When you find out your baby has died before birth, the world as you know it ceases to exist. You've likely never experienced anything like this, and it is normal for you to feel stunned, frightened, distraught, and completely unprepared.

Circle of care

In this book, Chapters 4 and 6 in particular, you'll find important information and support that can guide you as you prepare to labor, birth, and/or meet your baby. However, it is the rare parent who would feel ready, willing, or able to read *anything* during this traumatic time. Shocked, distressed, and bereft, you need far more than any book can provide, *especially* during the first hours and days of this journey.

In the beginning, the most important sources of information and support can be found in the circle of care that surrounds you. In recognition of this, the information in these pages is also intended to be useful to those who make up that circle—the caregivers who are trained to work with grieving parents during this time of greatest need, and the friends and family members who want to know how they can help. It is within the context of those relationships that you will receive compassionate, individualized, supportive bereavement care.

Key information

During the next few weeks or months, as your shock and disbelief subside, you may feel better equipped and able to pick up this book. In the meantime, here's an overview of information you might find helpful within the first few hours and days after finding out your baby has died. It is a list that you, or those around you, can refer to easily whenever you want to know or be reminded of key aspects to the early, and most overwhelming, part of your journey. Whenever you are ready for more information on any of these topics, you can turn to the relevant sections of this book.

- Finding out that your baby has died is a devastating and traumatic shock. It is natural to feel numb, disbelieving, confused, horrified, and uncertain how to proceed.
- Your baby's death is a deeply felt loss, as your bond grew strong before birth.
- Like most parents, you will likely want to spend time with your little one after birth. Discuss with your medical team the delivery methods that would best honor your wishes.
- If you aren't in labor yet, you may choose to be induced immediately, or you may decide to wait overnight or a day or so. As long as you're in good health, there are benefits to waiting, including acquiring information for the impending birth, gathering support people, and devising plans for spending time with your baby, making photographs, and collecting keepsakes.
- If you are carrying more than one baby, you can continue to carry the pregnancy to term for the benefit of any surviving baby(ies). After the birth, you'll be able to see and hold the baby who died.

- You may find it soothing to view labor and birth as sacred transitions and affirmations of motherhood. While laboring and birthing, you and your partner are claiming and honoring your role as parents to this child.
- You benefit from having caregivers who engage you in ongoing conversations about your feelings, ideas, questions, and concerns about spending time with your baby. It can also be helpful to hear what other parents have found meaningful and comforting.
- It's normal to feel fearful or nervous about meeting your baby. Your caregivers can describe and reassure you about your baby's appearance and assist you with the care you'd like to provide, at a pace that is comfortable for you.
- Examining, cuddling, and caring for your baby are ways you can express your love and nurturing. Later as you grieve and yearn to hold your baby, you can find comfort in these cherished memories of being with your little one.
- You can feel heartened when others treat your baby with respect and tenderness.
- If you take your baby home until burial or cremation, you get to immerse yourself in your parenting role and experience a tiny morsel of normalcy, which can be soothing.
- Whether in hospital or at home, having prolonged contact with your baby's body gives you the opportunity to gradually and truly experience it as a lifeless shell, which can help you part with it upon burial or cremation.
- Rituals such as providing care to the body, determining a final resting place, funeral or memorial service, and commemoration are all ways of parenting your baby.

- You will experience many layers of loss. It's normal to feel as if you've lost a part of yourself and your confidence in the future. You may also notice some people pulling away from you; they may be feeling awkward and unsure of what to say or do.
- Let family and friends know what kinds of support you need. Those who are truly devoted to your well-being will want to know.
- You and your partner will likely have very different ways of responding to your baby's death and birth. Remain kind and curious about your differences, and keep the lines of communication open.
- Feeling responsible for your baby's death is a natural part of being a parent, but it does not indicate that you are actually responsible.
- Stillbirth happens to many families every year. In fact, you may notice that when you open up about your experience, people will share their own, making you feel more normal and less alone.
- There is no right or wrong way to grieve. Your grief will be as unique and complex as you are.
- See your preoccupation with your baby as a natural part of grieving. Do what helps you remember and feel close to your baby.
- Be kind to yourself. Cry every tear. Take all the time you need.

Born Still

What is stillbirth?

Stillbirth is when a baby is born with no signs of life. Many stillborn babies die before labor has even started, and others die as they make their way into the world.

Medically speaking, the terms *miscarriage* and *stillbirth* differentiate between babies who die early in pregnancy versus those who die later in pregnancy. Governments vary in where they draw the line for the purpose of recording vital statistics, but typically when a baby is born still at or beyond 20 or 22 weeks' gestation or weighing at least 400 or 500 grams, the event is called a stillbirth. When the baby hasn't reached the required gestational age or weight, the event is called a miscarriage, a term that, for many parents, belittles the significance of their baby's life and death. Putting aside official definitions and medical terminology, in the hearts and minds of parents, stillbirth is when a beloved baby dies before he or she is born. This rings true particularly after the first few months of pregnancy, when the baby's body is formed and the mother's body must labor to give birth, even if by surgical procedure.

Annually in the United States, around 26,000 babies are stillborn after 19 weeks' gestation. And between 13 and 19 weeks' gestation, conservative estimates put the number of pregnancies that end in the death of a baby at over 65,000. So even though you may have never heard of stillbirth, it touches more than 90,000 families every year in this country alone.

Why did my baby die?

There are three types of problems that can cause a baby to be born still:

- Conditions in the baby—for example, infection or congenital abnormality that interferes with survival in the uterus or during delivery; the presence of more than one baby (twins, triplets, or higher-order multiples) also increases the risk.
- Conditions in the placenta or umbilical cord—for example, if the placenta starts to disintegrate or tear away from the uterine wall, or if the umbilical cord becomes constricted due to pinching, twisting, or disintegration.
- Conditions in the mother—for example, any illness, structure, trauma, or infection that interferes with her body's ability to maintain the pregnancy; any condition that inhibits the flow of oxygen or nutrients through the placenta; when a dangerous disease or drug crosses the placenta.

Unfortunately, for about half of all stillborn babies, no specific cause of death can be identified, even after autopsy. Any structural, bacterial, viral, genetic, gestational, physiological, or biochemical reason remains a mystery. This is largely because there is so much that is unknown about the human body and the miracle of pregnancy and birth.

How can I get answers as to why this happened?

If your pregnancy was identified as high risk, you may already have some clues as to what caused your baby's death. In some cases, the cause of death can be obvious, and you can ask your doctor for a thorough explanation.

If the cause of death isn't easily identified, you and your doctors will want follow-up testing. The doctor who attended the birth can examine the placenta and umbilical cord and may decide to send them to a pathology lab for a more thorough evaluation. You can make an appointment for a physical exam that might include evaluation of your blood, immune system, uterus and cervix, and other risk factors. The baby can have an autopsy.

Whether to consent to an autopsy for your baby's body is your decision. Your doctor might recommend it, you might want to know as much as possible about your baby's physiology, or you may consider it a chance to maybe find out what happened. You may be comforted by the thought that an autopsy could add to medical knowledge or yield information about your prospects for future pregnancies. Even if no specific cause of death is determined, you may appreciate knowing whether your baby was genetically or physically normal. On the other hand, you may feel that an autopsy, however gently done, is too invasive given that it offers no guarantee of revealing the cause of death.

Whether or not you consent to an autopsy, and even if your baby's cause of death is not able to be determined, if you feel so inclined, do ask questions. Ask your doctor or midwife how they think your baby died, and whether it could happen again. You can also ask for informative reading materials or websites. The value of any inquest is not to assign blame, but to understand the physiology. Getting this information can help you grasp the event, feel less vulnerable, and come to terms with what happened. Obtaining information is not morbid; it is *mastery*.

What if the cause of death can't be determined?

Without a specific reason for your baby's death, you may feel frustrated and confused by the lack of information. You may wonder obsessively, "What went wrong?" You may believe that having answers would help you to *understand* and perhaps avoid or prevent any recurrence.

In time, you will be able to come to terms with the unknown. Some parents come up with their own intuitive ideas about what happened, and many simply learn to accept that they cannot know for sure.

Even if a definitive cause of death is determined, your baby's death can seem beyond your understanding just the same. You may have questions that have no answers. You may review your actions and wonder, "What did I do?" or "What if I'd done things differently?" It is natural to ask, "Why me? Why my baby?" Alas, it's simply impossible to make sense of something so senseless.

Helen had a double knot in her umbilical cord. I struggled with the "what ifs" for months afterwards, and I think I always will, frustrated that she couldn't have been born when I went into labor at 34 weeks, when everything seemed to be okay. Obviously there are all kinds of complications that can go along with premature babies,

*too, but I've felt since then like she "knew" it was time for her to
come out at 34 weeks, and she was ready. But we did everything to
make sure that didn't happen. And she stayed in the womb where it
was supposedly "safe." Unfortunately, in Helen's case, it wasn't.*

—*Sally*

*We had autopsies done but they showed nothing. We know that
Mia was dead 24 to 72 hours and Grace for 12 to 24. I can't
believe that I didn't know when they died inside me. I had no
intuition and didn't even notice their movement stopping since they
were so still at the end. In my mind, I endlessly go over that Sunday
(when I lost my mucus plug) and wonder if Grace could have been
saved if I had gone into the hospital instead of phoning the doctor.
What if I hadn't rested so much? Maybe they would have been born
early enough to have lived. The questions are pointless but endless.*

*I know that having answers wouldn't take away the pain, but
it would be some comfort to understand it cognitively, even if we
never will spiritually know why such a tragic thing happened
to us.*

—*Darcie*

*There were no medical answers, nor any answers, which we found
so terribly frustrating. Why us? What did we do to deserve this
when Rachael was so loved and so wanted? Answers are not magic
potions with the ability to take away pain or bring our babies
back, but somehow we need them.*

Now, just one year later, I find myself no longer desperately searching for answers. The long and bumpy road through grief takes us to so many different emotions... I find I don't have room for guilt and blame. However, it is very hard to accept without reason that Rachael cannot be here with us on Earth. Not a day goes by that I don't ask myself "Why?" Just, "Why?"

—*Belinda*

Where do I go from here?

When your baby is stillborn, you are confronted with a traumatic and life-altering experience. Your grief knows no bounds and encompasses a bewildering mix of intense and painful emotions. Your toughest challenge is to adjust to *what is*, and let go of *what might have been*. But even as you grieve, you are gradually adjusting and reaching toward healing.

This small book is meant to help you get through the early days and weeks after your baby's death and birth. You'll find information and encouragement for enduring labor and birth, spending time with your little one, and making final plans for your baby's body. These sections can be particularly helpful if you've not yet given birth, but even if your baby has already been born and memorialized, reviewing these sections can help you process your experiences and your emotions, perhaps by jotting notes in a journal or in the margins. Throughout this book, you'll also find support around grieving, reassurance that your emotions are normal, and ideas for affirming your baby's life. For more information and support, turn to the additional resources listed in the back. For now, read the parts of this book that feel helpful to you. Come back to the passages that are particularly comforting and try reading other parts later. Take your time, and do what is best for you.

If reading this book moves you to cry, try to accept this reaction. These are healing tears of grief. They are also tears of health, courage, and strength that merge with those of other grieving parents. You are not alone.

3

Discovery

The nurse said I should still be feeling for the baby's movements, and counting them once in a while. That evening it seemed like I didn't remember the baby moving much during the day. I said something to Dan about it, but for some reason, neither of us was very worried about it. I think we'd heard something about how babies don't move as much toward the end, because they don't have as much room. Next morning I still didn't recall feeling any movement. For some reason I still wasn't really worried. I should've been.

That morning, I called the doctor. He told me to come in, and my mom drove me there. We got to the hospital; the nurse took me into a room and hooked me up to a monitor. She put the jelly on my stomach and started moving the monitor around. After a while, she started to look very concerned and went to get another nurse. The second nurse said she would set up the ultrasound machine and call the doctor. I was worried but not hysterical yet, because I don't think I could even grasp what was happening. I thought maybe when the doctor got there, he'd show the nurses what they were doing wrong—there had to be a heartbeat somewhere. My mom held my hand, but I wasn't going to cry yet. Then as soon as Dan walked in, he came over and hugged me, and I burst into tears. The doctor followed right behind... he took one look at the ultrasound monitor and simply said, "I'm sorry." You're sorry? In other words, your baby's dead. This couldn't be happening.

—*Sally*

A baby's death is often discovered during a routine exam, where the news is cruelly sudden and especially unexpected. Whether parents are blissfully naive or painfully aware of tragic possibilities, finding out is a terrible moment.

Since I was at 35 weeks, the doctor assured us that the girls would probably be just fine if born now. Then he did an ultrasound. He said he couldn't see Baby A's heart but said that their bones were calcified now and it was sometimes difficult to get a good picture. Then he grew ominously quiet as he continued to scan. In slow motion I grasped my husband's hand and started to understand that I couldn't see any movement at all. At all the other ultrasounds there was a limb, or a mouth, or something moving. "Are they dead?" I said, waiting for reassurance. Instead he said, "I don't see any movement, it doesn't look good." I remember that I kept insisting, "But not both of them." It had never occurred to me that we could lose both our twins... The shock was tremendous and protected us with numbness during that horrific day. The doctor sent us to the hospital where another ultrasound confirmed that our babies were dead. The technician cried with us as she led us to the childbirth center so I could be induced. We made phone calls to our families that broke their hearts.

—*Darcie*

I remember that I was lying in bed and the doctor wheeled in the ultrasound machine. Lavender was looking at the monitor, but I couldn't. Time stopped. It seemed like the longest moment in history. Everyone was quiet except the voice in my head screaming that no one was saying anything. Then the doctor said, "I am sorry,

Tanya. I cannot find a heartbeat." I can't possibly describe that feeling; like someone yanked my heart out and crushed it. I could hear myself sobbing, "No, no, tell me it is a dream! Please check again." But in my heart I knew it was true.

—Tanya

It was awful. Shock. I was numb. I was all alone. My husband, Chris, was at home with our two boys. With Emily, our third, I went to all the appointments without Chris. Up to this 15½-week appointment, we had no reason for concern. Mom and baby were doing well. I replay that day, February 5, over and over again, in my head. The ultrasound picture of Emily still. I thought she was sleeping at first. But then I realized that there was no heartbeat line. I knew what to look for and see. I had done these appointments many times before. And now, looking back, I took those heartbeats for granted. It felt and still does feel like a dream. I swore I just felt her move, out in the waiting room, right before I had been called back. I had just seen her at a previous appointment, dancing. I thought, "We are going to have a busy one on our hands."

—Anne

Disbelief

This horrible news can trigger a surreal sensation, such as being suspended in time and space, spiraling slowly out of control, or being thrust into a dreadful hallucination. At first, you might be a tad concerned, but you're not too worried because surely this isn't really happening and everything is fine. Then as more evidence is presented, you refuse to accept it. There must be some mistake. Operator error, faulty equipment, baby hiding. Finally, when the evidence is conclusive and you know it must be true because you trust the skill of your health care practitioners, you still resist because you cannot possibly take in the news. It's simply too much to bear and far too unreal for you to absorb. Even with tragedy looming, you may be calm, even hopeful, and appear unfeeling due to the power of shock and denial.

My husband and I went to our usual weekly checkup at the health center. During our visit the doctor checked for Laure's heartbeat. The week before she had a steady and strong heartbeat. I expected the same, but I knew something was wrong when the doctor quietly exited the room and entered with another doctor. After a few minutes they told us they couldn't find her heartbeat and that she had passed away. My husband immediately left the room. Their language became a bit blurry. I remember the doctors mentioning that my amniotic fluid was low and a series of other questions and observations. Then they asked me to go to the hospital. I was certain that when I got to the hospital they would find her heartbeat again, so I didn't allow the reality of the situation to affect me.

—Daniela

I still wanted this all to be a dream. But it wasn't. We had to get Emily out. She was gone. We had an ultrasound done every day to confirm that there was no heartbeat. I thought the medical staff may think I was in denial. Maybe. But I kept thinking, maybe there will be a miracle. Plus, in my head I was still almost 16 weeks' pregnant. And then I, her mother, who is supposed to protect her, is going to take her out before 40 weeks? Then at one of our last ultrasound appointments, the doctor said that there was water around her brain and her head was swollen. It finally sunk in. I realized that sadly, she was gone. Although I never doubted that she was with God from the beginning.

—Anne

Sometimes, a baby's death is not discovered until labor. If there is very little monitoring or if events take a sudden turn for the worse, a baby's death may not be confirmed until birth. If an emergency cesarean section is done in an attempt to save your baby's life (or your own), you may feel particularly scared or confused. It can seem especially cruel to go through such drastic measures only to have the baby declared dead upon delivery. The sudden shock can be overwhelming, and you simply cannot comprehend this reality.

In the eighteen minutes it had taken for the doctors to decide to operate, anesthetize me, and carry out a cesarean, my baby had been born. He had been born, but he did not wake up.

I don't think I took it in when they told me. I vaguely recall screaming "No!" but I don't really remember much of anything. I'd been given a lot of morphine. I know Mum gave me Finley to hold, but I must have fallen asleep again. I have photographs of that first morning, not memories.

—Mel

However and whenever your baby's death is confirmed, finding out is traumatic and sends you reeling.

Never, not even for a moment, did we think that anything could go so horribly wrong at the end of my uneventful, peaceful, so-called textbook pregnancy. But it did. At 39 weeks, without warning or reason, my placenta completely detached, causing massive hemorrhage and depriving our precious baby daughter of oxygen. Even as we rushed to the hospital, I knew something was very wrong with me, but surely our baby was going to be fine. We'd made it to the end. We were ready and very excited. Our baby had taken so long to happen... certainly that was a big enough test. But our precious baby died... and so did our souls.

—Belinda

Stillbirth is a terrible, unbelievable violation of your expectations. You were eagerly planning to say hello to your baby, and instead you are forced to say good-bye. A happy beginning becomes a sad ending. Birth becomes death. That is *not* the way it's supposed to be.

Premonitions

After the baby's death is discovered, the mother might recall a lack of movement, an unusual flurry of activity, or "an odd feeling." But for many mothers, even in hindsight, there was not a clue.

Once I'd got past the 12 weeks milestone, I happily assumed everything would go smoothly. I never considered the possibility that something could happen later on. Getting pregnant and carrying a healthy baby to term should be easy. I mean, it's the most natural thing in the world, isn't it?

—Mel

At the other extreme, some mothers have strong premonitions, such as dreams, physical sensations, or uneasiness that something will go wrong. When their baby's fate is discovered, these mothers see their intuitions as foreshadowing.

Since this was my second pregnancy, I was really expecting everything to be fine. But this baby moved very little. The first time the baby moved, I thought, "Are you growing to live or living till you die?" I was horrified that thought crossed my mind.

—Leah

You always worry about your baby, to some degree, while pregnant. But with Emily, it was almost always an unsettling feeling. Often since our baby's death, I have thought, "Was that God preparing me? Us?"

—Anne

All of my dreams were vividly colored in red, as if by blood. One night, I dreamed of contractions and death. I would soon learn that our baby had died—I am certain on this night. I have been so disappointed in myself for not consciously knowing the moment of Gabriel's death.

—Mary

If you had no premonitions or intuitions or if you didn't notice any signs, this bears *no* reflection on your maternal instinct or your ability to protect your baby. Not knowing there was a problem or being unaware of precisely when your baby died is *not* a mark of failure. How could you have known? Even mothers who have strong premonitions couldn't prevent their baby's death or know when their baby died. Even if you could have a Plexiglas window and constant fetal monitoring, there are considerable limits to what you can do and know about the baby(ies) in your womb.

With my first two pregnancies I felt "green" for the first trimester, never beyond week 13. With this pregnancy, I felt much worse and for a longer period. I had always felt strong fetal movement at early stages with my boys. With this baby, something was different, unnervingly quiet and slow. I shared my concerns with nurses and my doctor. I don't remember feeling heard.

As I readied myself for an amniocentesis, I remember bending over and actually feeling a small round shape on my right side. This was my baby's head, I am sure, no longer cushioned safely by amniotic fluid. Brian took me to the doctor's office. We looked at beautiful pictures of healthy babies in photograph books as we waited. I am certain I smiled. We walked in, I lay down, my belly was jelled, and a new sonographer began. I knew immediate fear. Our baby's head was no longer smooth and round, but more oblong, and I could see his head sutures were misshapen. The sonographer looked and looked and asked daring questions, "Have you felt any movement?" Yes, I am sure I had, I am sure, but she began to cry and told me she couldn't see my baby's heart beating. Our baby was dead. The world slipped out from under my feet and has yet to return to me as I knew it.

—Mary

Forewarning

While many parents have no warning, no risk factors, no trouble detected until death has occurred, some parents are forewarned during pregnancy. A baby who is prenatally diagnosed with a life-limiting condition might not survive long enough to be born alive. Other babies are in danger due to maternal complications, and some pregnancies hold a high level of risk, such as with multiple babies or the position of the placenta.

> *When the baby's kidneys were showing signs of stress at my first ultrasound, my doctor seemed to blow it off. I was under 35, healthy, and had already successfully delivered a baby—the fact that this baby was dying in utero from a rare genetic disorder never crossed his mind. I didn't fit the "profile" for a troubled pregnancy.*
>
> *A level-two ultrasound was done and they discovered that the baby's kidneys were failing... When I asked what was going on, was the baby okay, the doctor replied, "Our counselor will explain it to you." I knew that counselors are involved when the news is bad. I put my hand over my mouth and began sobbing. My husband blocked the door and asked the doctor what was going on. The doctor said something about "compatible/not compatible with life." What was in my womb was questionable [incompatible] with life? For six months we had been expecting a baby and now we had an "incompatible fetus." My maternal pride was crushed. In an instant we were no longer treated as expectant parents but medical anomalies. We got another perinatologist.*

—Leah

With pregnancy complications, parents benefit from supportive care as they face grief even before their baby's birth. Sometimes labor is induced early to increase the parents' chance of greeting a live newborn. But not all babies make it. Even when a baby is clearly at risk, stillbirth is still an unbearable and shocking turn of events.

4

Birth

After the baby's death is confirmed, especially if the mother is not yet in labor, she may feel overwhelmed by the thought of continuing to carry a baby who is no longer alive. Some mothers want labor to be induced as soon as possible. Others want to put off delivery, knowing that it will lead to separation from the baby. Still others feel torn. There's just no "great" way to proceed.

Wait or deliver as soon as possible?

The nurse practitioner eventually said she was so very sorry and went on to ask me, did I want to deliver right away? Or did I want to let nature take its course, since I was so close to my due date anyway, and because I was also already 3 cm dilated? I was in complete shock . . . I could not think . . . I could not form words or think of questions to ask her.

Honestly, when a bereaved, in-shock mom has just been given this type of horrific news without further explanation as to what the benefits might be in delivering right away versus waiting to deliver, I strongly feel that most bereaved moms would more than likely choose to deliver right away, due to the fight-or-flight response. And this was exactly what I did—I chose to deliver right away.

The nurse practitioner made me feel like I was making the right decision when she said to me, "If I was in your situation I would do the same thing."

Now that I know what I know, but obviously didn't know then, I would have waited to deliver—at least waited one day, anyway.

—Lori

Waiting can have its benefits. Some mothers want time to center themselves before entering the rigors of labor. Waiting even a day or just overnight can let you make special preparations for commemorating this baby, such as acquiring infant clothing and blankets, gathering together friends and family to meet your baby, getting out your camera or finding someone else to take photographs, and considering ways to be present with and provide care for your baby's body. (For more on this, see Chapter 6, Affirming Your Baby.)

I felt like the world was spinning with all of the quick decisions we had to make. I remember saying to my mom, who arrived first at the doctor's office, "I would like to go to church tomorrow and pray. And meet with a priest." And Chris and I did. I am so glad that we did.

—Anne

Furthermore, a baby's death in and of itself does not pose an immediate danger to the mother's health. And as long as you are physically comfortable and have no signs of fever, infection, or illness, your doctor can advise you on how long you can wait with your baby inside you.

One reason to not wait too long is that within 24 to 48 hours after death in the womb, most babies' skin starts to visibly change, with tiny, reddish, peeling patches beginning to form here and there. After a bit longer, death also affects the structure of the baby's face and body, meaning that both the tissue and bones are not as firm, but start to soften or become loose. Many parents hold expectations about their baby's physical appearance, particularly the face, and envision a cherubic newborn with rosy cheeks and perfect lips. When a baby dies before birth, you may be concerned about your baby looking far different from what you've been expecting or envisioning.

It's natural to feel afraid or nervous about seeing your baby. You may be fearful of losing that cherubic image in your mind, and you certainly don't want a dreadful image to be your enduring memory of this child. But imagination can be far more horrifying than reality, and parents are generally relieved at how "normal" their baby looks and feel grateful for the opportunity to hold their infant in their arms and express their love.

There is no right or wrong decision about how and when—or even whether—to spend time with your baby after birth. You may want to see and touch your baby right away, or you may prefer your newborn handed to you after being cleaned and wrapped in a blanket. Perhaps you simply want to hold your little one without looking. You can always ask someone to describe your baby so you can feel reassured and know what to expect. (You can also be informed by an ultrasound scan before the birth.) Eventually, at the time of your choosing, you can gaze upon your son or daughter, be present with your little one, and honor your baby's body. Know that most parents are surprised by how quickly they are able to see past softened skin or peeling patches or any deformities and just see the beauty of their child.

The perinatologist we chose was wonderful and used ultrasound to familiarize us with our baby's abnormalities. This helped brace us for the things about Adam that were unique. But the funny thing was, when he was born, we really took to heart what was familiar about him, like the trademark family ears. Yes, he had a lot of anomalies, but seen through the eyes of love, he was just beautiful.

—Leah

If you are pregnant with multiple babies, waiting can mean many days, weeks, or months of carrying your babies closer to term to benefit your surviving baby(ies). To carry life and death together in your womb can seem extremely challenging. You may fear that none of your babies will survive. When you feel movement, you may worry about the deceased baby being jostled. In anticipation of the birth, you may fear seeing a baby who has been dead for a while, and yet feel ashamed for being afraid of your little one.

The bottom dropped out of our hopes at 23 weeks. Our ultrasound technician told us she could not detect a heartbeat on the [smaller] twin. She quickly left to get my doctor as Ron and I sat in shocked silence. Somehow I managed to get through the ultrasound that confirmed the other twin was alive and appeared fine. My doctor answered my questions and tried to console us with the knowledge that this situation would greatly improve the odds of the survivor going to term. The shock of hearing I would carry both babies so long was just overwhelming.

In the next 16 weeks, I ran the gamut of emotions. Mostly, we felt saddened to lose a baby who had struggled so hard to live. I had grown very attached to them both and loved to see them bat at each other each time we peeked at them during the ultrasounds. For the first few weeks, I could barely stand to look at my abdomen, because all I could think about was Robert. Until the amniotic fluid level on the surviving twin stabilized I could barely feel his movements, which left me with a constant feeling of impending doom. It took us months to get over the feeling that the whole pregnancy was doomed.

The two weeks prior to labor were spent getting mentally prepared for delivery. Frankly, Ron and I were scared . . . what would Robert look like? Would we be repulsed, and worse yet, what if we couldn't look?

—*Vicki*

All of these protective feelings for your babies are natural expressions of parental devotion. You may benefit from keeping a journal of your experiences, thoughts, worries, and feelings of love during the remainder of this pregnancy. Your doctor may suggest performing an ultrasound just before the birth to give you an idea of what to expect. You can also contact a bereaved parents support group and ask to talk to other parents who have been through similar experiences. They can help you set aside your fears and prepare for birthing and meeting all your babies.

Robert delivered in the placenta. Before long we were in a private room with both boys snuggled on my lap. Seeing Robert was not the sad, scary experience I had feared. It just felt so good to see and hold him. As I had been told to expect, he was very small and rather flat from spending 16 weeks next to his growing brother. . . . Finally

*we were free of the fear. . . . We took video and pictures of all of us
together, baptized Robert that evening, and said good-bye.*

—*Vicki*

Whatever your circumstances, you benefit from the sensitive
care of your doctor or midwife and the presence of a nurse who can
anticipate, guide, offer suggestions, and bear witness as you greet
your newborn. Besides reassuring you about your baby's appearance,
your caregivers can help you create a supported way of holding your
baby (for example, swaddled, a firm hold on the back of your baby's
head and neck), and assist you with the care you would like to provide, all at a pace that is comfortable for you.

Whether you're waiting a few hours or have many months
to go, you may find it helpful to reset your frame of mind from
dramatic visions of death to the fact that you are still sheltering this
little baby. And when your baby is born, you will look through eyes
of love and see how precious your baby is.

Anticipating labor and birth

Knowing your baby has died, especially if you're the mother, it is
natural to dread labor and fear that you might go out of your mind.
In an effort to try to find the "easy" way out, some mothers beg for a
cesarean section, only to be told that vaginal delivery is much safer.
And when a C-section is deemed necessary, this surgery can feel
particularly invasive and burdensome as it doesn't benefit the baby.
In any case, the entire process can seem like it will be an exercise in
endurance with no reward.

We were in such shock we didn't even know how to react. The doctor said they could start inducing me right now. What? You mean I have to go through labor to have a baby who isn't even alive? Dan said something like, "You're not serious—can't you do a C-section or something?" And the doctor kind of snapped back something like, "Of course not, that would be unnecessary surgery." Oh, of course. Why couldn't we be that logical? There were many people who were incredibly helpful through our heartbreaking experience, but that doctor wasn't one of them.

—*Sally*

When the OB explained that I would have to deliver the babies, I was horrified. To go through the pain of childbirth for nothing seemed unbearably cruel. He offered us the option of waiting until the next day, but it couldn't be over fast enough for me. The hours passed in a haze of painkillers and disbelief. I literally felt out of my body when talking with the rabbi about funeral arrangements or asking my sister to repack my bag to remove the baby things and bring it to the hospital.

—*Darcie*

Somehow we got home, though I have no idea how Lavender managed to drive the car. They gave me sleep meds and antinausea meds but I did not sleep. I do not know how I got through that night.

—*Tanya*

Depending on your baby's gestational age and your medical history, your doctor may offer different options—to wait until labor starts naturally, to induce labor, or, particularly with earlier gestations, to surgically intervene, such as with dilation and extraction (D&E), which mechanically removes the baby after medically expanding the cervix. As for most parents, it is likely important to you to keep your baby's body whole and spend time with your little one after birth, so talk with your medical team about the options that would best honor your wishes.

I was informed hours before I was to go into the operating room to have the D&E that our baby would not be a whole body. That our baby would be in parts. That was hard to accept. Then I thought, Well, it will be like she is a soldier coming home from war. Still, I could not do it. I wanted to come back next week. There was only so much I could handle. We found out on a Tuesday that our baby had died. This was a Friday. Our nurse said, "You can always try to labor and deliver, though there is no guarantee as to how long that could take." It did not matter. It was an answer to my prayer. As sad as this situation was, I wanted to labor and deliver, just as I had with our other two children. I wasn't pretending that our baby might be alive. I knew she was gone. But I wanted to try and have her whole. There was still a possibility that doing it this way she might not come out whole. But I wanted to try and hope.

—Anne

When you contemplate the prospect of a vaginal birth, consider this: for a woman, laboring and birthing are sacred acts that affirm you as the mother of this baby. If you are the attentive partner, your support affirms your role as father or coparent of this baby. For both of you, birthing is a rite of passage that you, as parents, still get to experience. And if you endure a surgical delivery, this too has its challenges, and you will have earned your stripes as parents.

Ask if you can meet with your hospital's bereavement coordinator, or contact a bereaved parents support group or organization to find the support and counsel of a bereaved parents advocate. You might also be able to enlist a bereavement doula, who can be your companion and advocate as you labor and greet your newborn. Any specially trained caregiver can advise you on how to proceed with the birth, how to cope with labor, and how to consider spending time with your precious baby. (See Chapter 6: Affirming Your Baby.)

I remember someone saying that they wanted to induce me the next day. I said that I didn't know if I could do it, that they might need to cut the baby out of me. . . . I called my friend Joy who has also lost a baby. She said that laboring could be part of the healing and that I needed to labor for this baby.

—*Tanya*

If I could have had a do-over, I would have contacted the A.M.E.N.D. Baby Loss Support Group leader in my area and had her meet with me and my family to help us emotionally and physically, help prepare us for what was to come, and help bring some calm, wise, compassionate guidance and support to us in our time of great need.

—*Lori*

Tolerating labor and birth

For many mothers, shock, denial, and numbness persist throughout labor. You may assume or wonder if your baby will come out kicking and screaming and prove everyone wrong. In a way, this disbelief can be a blessing. As Daniela recalls, "At the hospital and during labor I think I went into survival mode. Looking back I may have been in shock and in denial. I felt inside of me that she may still be alive."

Another blessing is the people who rally around you during this crisis. As you labor, you can lean on the skilled care and compassion of your nurses, midwives, and doctors. You can rely on anesthetists to administer palliative care to ease your physical pain. You can share this experience with your partner. You can draw on the love of your family and friends, as they keep you in their thoughts and prayers. You can depend on your religious faith or spiritual beliefs.

I felt so lost. We had taken hypnobirthing classes, but all the exercises and CDs were about picturing a healthy baby and birth. I felt that all my tools had left me.

My midwife says I was an Amazon, but I didn't feel powerful. I felt empty and torn apart. With the Pitocin I had a very fast first stage of labor (maybe eight hours, with about four of those in active labor) and then I only pushed for forty-seven minutes. I was so determined to get the baby out.

By the time I was in active labor, many, many people were sending strength. I do not think I could have gotten through labor without this. At times I thought I heard people singing. I felt moments of calm in between moments of fear and pain.

—Tanya

At 24 weeks, I was induced while Adam was still alive. If he survived birth, he would be given directly to us, to die in our arms...

My labor was so different from my firstborn. Ryan was constantly monitored and the excitement grew as the delivery time grew close. The medical staff and my husband cheered during the pushing and after he was born. This time, when Adam's time grew near and I felt the urge to push, I kept calling out, "Help me, help me," part of it from the physical pain but most of it from the pain of knowing it was time to say good-bye. I cried for God to show mercy; I didn't know if I could watch my baby die. Adam was stillborn.

—Leah

Whether you're still numb with shock or in emotional agony or somewhere in between, you can hold on to the knowledge that this ordeal is temporary, with a finite number of contractions and pushes. Each contraction you feel is one more contraction you can check off as "done." Also, the mind has a way of protecting itself. You may find yourself zoning out or calming down in response to feeling overwhelmed. It can help to have a focal point, such as a soothing mantra, a peaceful image in your mind, or an object in the room. You can even focus on greeting your newborn and request that your baby be met with rejoicing upon birth. Even though this birth can be a tremendously difficult experience, you will prevail.

As I kept pushing, trying to get my baby's body all the way out, I found that without realizing it, I would zone out on the fluorescent lights above me. And then the reality of the situation would force me out of my zoning out... it would hit me once again what was truly happening here and I would cry and breathe hard... and then I couldn't take it anymore and would zone out on the fluorescent lights again. Back and forth... back and forth, I kept doing this, and I guess that I somewhat coped during the delivery.

—Lori

During labor I anxiously anticipated her birth. What would she look like? Did she have my hair, his eyes? Was she tall? Was she chubby? I didn't want anyone in the room to cry or look sad. For me her birth was still a joyous event to be celebrated.

—Daniela

Labor went quickly. I had an epidural put in place. My water broke on its own. There were no signs of labor up to this point, so we had medicine placed internally, inside of me, to get labor underway. Emily arrived quickly, too. My husband, Chris, was actually on the couch when she came out of me. She was born at 11:50pm. It was sad, but wonderful. I kept saying to her, "You are amazing."

—Anne

Lavender was incredible. She was able to take the affirmations from the hypnobirthing class and re-word them so that I could stay focused during pushing. Though I had an epidural I still felt every contraction and was able to push effectively.

I will always remember the feeling of his heavy body sliding silently out of me, just like the feeling of all that amniotic fluid pouring out when my membranes were ruptured. There was this moment where I took a breath and tried to prepare myself to look at my child. Lavender encouraged me to see the baby. "The baby is beautiful." He was. As we cried, held him, and gazed as his sweet little face, I had a moment of utter peace. I think it must have been grace.

—Tanya

5

The Depth of Your Loss

Looking at Helen, Dan and I both felt that "instant" love that everybody tells you about, but that you can't understand until it happens to you. Our hearts were broken, but one thing was undeniable—we had become parents.

—*Sally*

When a baby is stillborn, a common misunderstanding is that parents won't feel much of a loss, "since they never had a chance to bond with the baby." Even you may be surprised at the intensity of your grief. But you grieve intensely because your bond to this baby had already deepened throughout your pregnancy.

Bonding is not something that begins at birth. It is a process that can start even before conception as you dream of having a baby someday. After your pregnancy is confirmed, even if unplanned, you can start envisioning yourself as a parent to this particular child. You can talk to your baby, stroke the blooming belly, collect infant clothing and supplies, and pick out names. You may never get the chance to hold this baby alive in your arms, but you certainly held this baby alive in your body, in your future imaginings, and in your heart.

Oh, I was so happy. My dream had come true. I was finally a mother, the only thing I had continued to dream about since I was a little girl rocking dollies to sleep.

—*Belinda*

*Twins! Wow . . . this is unreal. The first thought I recall is that we
had to go out and buy one of those strollers-built-for-two. How
ironic. I've just been told we are expecting twins and all I can think
of is, should we get the side-by-side model or the front-and-back
model? . . . It's never too early to get these details worked out.*

—Ron

*I craved vegetables this time. With the boys, fruit. I thought, Maybe
we do have a little girl on the way.*

—Anne

*We went to our Blessingway—a ceremony honoring a woman
becoming a mother—hosted by my friend Meg. Lavender and I
read to each other what we had written about family and honoring each other as coparents and partners. And I wanted to honor
Lavender as the mother she already was. . . . Lavender and I were
given beads, sang songs, did a belly cast of my pregnant belly, and
had our feet washed in a bath of sea salt, seaweed, and flowers. It
was exquisitely beautiful.*

—Tanya

Others may wonder why you grieve, "since you never got
to know this child." But in many heartfelt ways, you were becoming acquainted with this baby well before birth. As the weeks and
months wore on, you were able to feel the life unfolding inside you.
You could feel your baby's kicks and hiccups. Perhaps you saw ultrasound images. After birth, you may notice a family resemblance or
endearing qualities. While you don't know if this child would have
been athletic, scholarly, artistic, dreamy, or mechanically inclined,

you counted on having the chance to find out. And even with all the unknowns, you cherish this child.

We saw our baby for the first time on a rainy Halloween evening. He was still too little to determine gender. Looking directly at his picture on the monitor, Brian said, "I have fallen in love."

—*Mary*

Layers of loss

It wasn't just the loss of Oren. Yes, that was excruciating. It was. But there are other losses too, those for which you don't get sympathy cards. I can picture one card now. On the front, a little white calla lily with a raindrop perched on a petal. It would say, "With sympathy," and inside something like, "My thoughts are with you as you struggle to rebuild your self-esteem and feel at home in your new post-trauma body."

—*Tanya*

When your baby dies, you experience many layers of loss. Your hopes and dreams for the near future come crashing down. Perhaps you'd hoped for an easy labor and planned for a natural birth, but now you are consenting to induction and painkillers. You'd expected to greet a squawking newborn instead of dead silence. You'd envisioned reveling in maternal pride instead of wondering if your body is an agent of harm. You'd imagined sharing your joy rather than withdrawing into sorrow.

Knowing that our baby had died, the birth experience was agony and completely opposite to everything I had learned, hoped, planned, and imagined. It was so very quiet. Our baby wasn't crying. She lay so still. We felt so alone.

—Belinda

You may also grieve for the distant future. Visions of first smiles, first teeth, first steps, and first days at school go up in smoke. In all, you grieve deeply for what might have been.

Today at work, a coworker announced with joy the birth of their daughter. In my heart I was happy for these new parents. But my heart is still broken as we just delivered a baby boy, Adam John. A cute little kid who looked full of mischief and couldn't wait to get in trouble with his older brother. Splash in mud puddles, pull the dog's tail, eat cookies before dinner . . . I will never be able to teach him how to shoot a hockey puck, or to douse a spinnaker sail in a yacht race, or to scare Mom with a batch of night crawlers, or to teach him about more important things like I'm sorry or I love you.

—Fred

There are also losses inherent to stillbirth. You may wish you could have seen your baby alive in your arms, even for a moment. Many parents of stillborn babies speak of their sorrow about never seeing their baby's eyes or never feeling their baby's grasp. You may regret that your baby never felt your kisses, never heard the loving words you spoke after the birth. You may cringe at how quickly your baby's body turns cold, and how you don't get an official birth certificate. These missed opportunities and acknowledgments must be grieved as well.

There are losses that come from enduring crisis. You may lose faith in modern medicine or obstetric care. You may lose touch with some friends, and some of your relationships with relatives might change. (See "Isolation" later in this chapter.) Your relationship with your partner may require learning new communication skills. Some changes will be for the better, but any change is hard when you're distressed.

Finally, you may feel as if you've lost a part of yourself. This baby is an extension of your love, your genetic perpetuation, your wishes, your talents, your being. Primed to protect and take care of your little one, you now question your identity as a parent. Particularly as a mother, your emptiness is deeply felt, since you carried your baby inside your body and every cell of your being yearns to nurture this child. You may struggle with body image and feel rudderless on an open sea.

This has been a long and lonely trek. Gabriel has brought us into depths within ourselves that were unimaginable. We will never be who we were before his poignant life.

—*Mary*

What does it mean to be a mother now, when I have had a miscarriage and a stillborn son? And how do I live in a body that has been the whole world to a small boy and been his coffin as well?

—*Tanya*

Multiple babies

With multiples, there are more layers of loss. If you were pregnant with twins, triplets, or more, you know the joy and anticipation of multiple babies. There is something special about multiples, and having them can be a source of pride and wonder. When some or all of your babies die, you also grieve for the lost chance to raise those babies together. You may wish you could watch them grow up as a set and enjoy their special bond. Your heartstrings are tugged every time you see other multiples and imagine "what if."

If more than one baby has died, you have more than one loss to bear. In addition, unless all your babies are stillborn, multiple babies mean multiple realities, perhaps including hospitalization, treatment decisions, and homecoming. A surviving baby means acknowledging life and death simultaneously. It can be quite a challenge to feel joyful and devastated at the same time.

This moment [of birth] is the epitome of bittersweet. On one hand, we are celebrating the birth of our new son, Cody Alexander; however, we are also mourning the loss of son Robert Evan. Although I had three months to prepare for this moment, the tears were quick to flow from a well I thought I had buried deep inside. Over the last few weeks I had been so careful not to allow myself to think of this moment and when it came, I found myself quite unprepared for it. And the tears flowed—the uncontrollable sobbing brought on by a loss I never felt before.

—Ron

Isolation

Back at the office, nobody said anything. No "Congratulations!" No "I'm sorry." I was on my own. Oh sure, the company president said, "It must be God's will to have something like this happen to you." I might try that the next time we lose a large account.

        —Fred

Expectations can be very cruel. Lots of people who had been so caring stopped phoning, even stopped talking to us. . . . When you feel so different anyway, the last thing you need is being made to feel like a leper. It was then that I realized that expectations were obviously not a good thing. I didn't want to be angry and bitter. So I learned that, if someone said something kind, then great, and if not, well, I didn't expect it, anyway.

        —Belinda

    Feelings of isolation are very common for grieving parents. People naturally shy away from discussing the death of someone's loved one. Even your health care practitioners can feel at a loss for words or not know how to respond.

I still do not quite understand this, but when I found out that our baby had died, the two ultrasound technicians left me. I felt so alone as it was. I swung open the door, and called out after them (or anyone). I said, "You cannot leave me alone. I was just told that my baby died." I probably startled a few in that office that day, but

I needed someone. Anyone to just sit with me until my mother or husband could arrive and be with me.

—Anne

Your closest relatives, friends, and neighbors may not comprehend that you cannot and must not forget. Some may discount your grief with "Just have another baby" in a misguided attempt to make you feel better. Others may believe that you should be able to get "back to normal" in a matter of weeks. You may have friends who withdraw due to feeling awkward and not wanting to say anything for fear of upsetting you. Others may try to avoid you and your baby's death in order to avoid the reality that bad things happen to good people—and that children (even theirs) can die.

When my husband and I came home from the hospital, my mother was at our house caring for our two-year-old. She gave me a hug and said, "It's over, no one will ever bring it up." But I needed to bring it up. One of our children had just died!

—Leah

This is silent and painful. I can't tell of my wife's gallant labor or how beautiful our son was. Only those who have experienced loss want to know. As my office became electrified with this new father's story about his daughter's birth, I feel strange. We just had a child and nobody cares. They said he should take some time off to help his wife. They thought that since my child is dead I should get back to work. How unfair. My wife needs support and I would like to be there for her.

—Fred

As people turn away, you may believe that you are the only one who thinks about, misses, and honors your stillborn baby. You may wonder if they even care about you or your baby. This only adds to your pain. Or they may marvel at how "great" you're doing, which only demonstrates that they are completely disconnected from the wild storm raging inside you.

> *It's a struggle when people are so nice all the time. It's not that they're usually unpleasant, of course. It's just that now it's a different sort of kindness, and I find it hard to handle. Everyone keeps saying how brave we are. It doesn't feel like they're talking about us at all. This isn't bravery. It's not even coping.*
>
> —Mel

Even in a support group, you may be rebuffed by bereaved parents who disagree with any agonizing medical decisions you made or disapprove of the way you live your life. As Tanya says, "You are so incredibly vulnerable in the wake of stillbirth that it is hard to deal with judgment or perceived judgment at the same time."

Raising a surviving multiple can feel especially isolating. Your surviving baby doesn't erase your need to grieve for the baby who died, but friends and family may try to get you to focus only on the living. While people are just trying to console you, they are not supporting your need to grieve and leave you wondering if you're the only one who thinks of the baby who was born still.

While feelings of isolation are all too common, you can find people to be there for you. Some friends will be able to support you after you coach them on what you need. Don't expect them to read your mind. Let them know what you find helpful and that it's therapeutic to talk and cry about your baby. Mention that you value the friends who can listen and accept, without trying to "fix." Remind them that the most comforting words are "I'm sorry."

In addition, you may notice that when you open up about your baby's stillbirth, other people may seem to come out of the woodwork to share their own experiences of stillbirth, making you feel less alone. If you can, attend a well-run support group, either in person or online, so that you can meet other bereaved parents who are accepting and compassionate. Those who truly understand can be a lifeline for you.

Physical recovery

Physical recovery following stillbirth may be straightforward, or it may be compounded by physical trauma, including pregnancy complications, induced labor, difficult birth, or an emergency cesarean section. Recovery can also be compounded by the emotional trauma you're experiencing. In your shock and despair, you may not be able to direct adequate attention to self-care or find the energy to tend to your recuperation from pregnancy and birth. Grief itself can cause sleep disruption, fatigue, anxiety, and a faltering appetite, which are not conducive to healing. Without a baby in your arms, there is little to soothe your postpartum pains. As a result, physical recovery can take longer than expected. Certainly, if you have any signs of fever, tenderness, redness, or unusual swelling in your abdomen, around tears or stitches, or on your breasts, call your midwife or doctor, as you may be fighting a serious infection that warrants prompt medical attention.

It may help you to have extra postpartum checkups, perhaps one before the typical six weeks and another one a few months down the road. These exams can reassure you that your body is recovering properly. You can also ask questions and get guidance about continued recovery, sexual intimacy, physical activity, nutrition, and future pregnancies. Your doctor or midwife should also inquire about your grief and emotional coping and refer you to additional sources of support. When you make the appointments, ask that your chart be flagged regarding your bereavement, request the first appointment of the morning or afternoon, and ask to be ushered straight to an exam room upon arrival. These measures serve to spare you the sight of pregnant women and babies or the chore of informing practitioners of your baby's death.

The postpartum period is normally a time when the mother's partner, friends, and family pitch in and help. Even though you don't have your baby, you still deserve postpartum tender loving care. Let your partner, close friends, and available relatives assist you in tending to your medical and physical needs. They can rejuvenate you with everything from intimate postpartum care to meal preparation to taking on chores to accompanying you on therapeutic forays to your favorite park. In the process they benefit from knowing their assistance is of real comfort to you.

You might also consider hiring home health care, or more specifically, a postpartum doula, trained to help women and families following childbirth. You may even be able to find a bereavement doula. This extra support can be priceless.

Breast care

For most mothers, even when a baby is stillborn, the process of giving birth stimulates hormones that tell the body to make breast milk. Of all the postpartum issues bereaved mothers experience, dealing with engorged breasts is perhaps the most difficult. Breast milk is a strong affirmation of your motherhood and a reassuring sign that your body is capable of nourishing a baby, but it is an especially cruel reminder that there's no baby to feed.

Milk usually comes in three to five days after a baby is born, and the mother's breasts will feel engorged and perhaps leak milk. (Some mothers' bodies skip this engorgement period, so don't be alarmed either way.) If you experience painful pressure, swelling, or lumpiness, you can relieve it by expressing a little milk every few hours by hand or using a manual breast pump. Leave in as much milk as is comfortable, because a chemical present in the retained milk signals the milk glands to depress production, and over time your supply will naturally fade away.

Other measures that relieve discomfort include cold compresses and ibuprofen or acetaminophen. A warm shower might induce milk leakage and reduce painful pressure. While a well-fitting bra can help too, binding breasts is an ineffective folk remedy that might intensify your pain and increase the risk of infection.

There is a different option that some bereaved mothers find therapeutic: expressing and donating their milk to a human milk bank. These banks make breast milk available to sick and premature infants whose mothers cannot provide this vital nourishment. Donating is a generous and compassionate act. For a bereaved mother, donation can feel like a meaningful way to turn a negative experience into a positive one. You can donate expressed milk in honor of your baby.

If you'd like to explore this option, a midwife, nurse, or lactation consultant can show you how to pump efficiently, and the human milk bank nearest you will provide instructions on collection, storage, donation and if necessary can arrange for free overnight transportation. For locations, visit the nonprofit Human Milk Banking Association of North America at www.hmbana.org.

Regardless of when and how you do it, reducing your milk supply can be an emotional process, so take your time, seek extra support, and be gentle with yourself.

> *I donated his milk to a local milk bank for three months and got to know the twins who were the primary recipients. My milk even went to help the newest baby of the woman who had started the milk bank years ago when her son was stillborn! Talk about full circle.*
>
> *—Tanya*

6

Affirming Your Baby

A neighbor once said, "What a waste, to go through labor and delivery for nothing." I was furious—Adam was not for nothing. He is part of the fabric woven into my life that makes me what I am today. I'm proud of the little fellow.

—Leah

Affirming your baby's existence and importance can ease the trauma of stillbirth. Affirming your baby can include:

- remembering the pregnancy, labor, and birth
- seeing and holding your baby after birth
- having family and friends meet and hold your baby
- naming your baby
- having your baby blessed
- collecting keepsakes such as photos, footprints, locks of hair, and infant clothing
- bathing and dressing your baby
- taking your baby home
- contemplating burial or cremation
- holding a funeral or memorial service
- visiting where the body is buried or where the ashes are scattered or held

These are all ways to acknowledge that your baby is important to you. Having memories of your baby's existence and appearance can help you comprehend, and even identify for whom you grieve. Seeing and holding your baby can make her or his existence more real. Saving keepsakes can make your good-byes more gradual and provide a means for sharing memories. Taking your baby home can yield priceless memories and the gift of time with your little one. Rituals like baptism and funeral help others recognize the value of your baby, understand the depth of your loss, and share your sorrow.

When my son was stillborn, I did two things I'd never have imagined doing a day earlier. I loved a dead body. And I wrote. Both were flailing attempts to change the horror that every parent of a stillborn baby lives with: If no one knew this child, then no one will remember him, and if no one remembers him, then he'll have left the world without a trace.

—*Elizabeth*

Overall, affirming your baby honors this little life and offers you the opportunity to affirm your identity as a mother or father to this child. Ultimately, affirming your baby can make your grief feel more manageable.

Being with your baby

It's natural to feel shocked or distressed at the thought of seeing and touching your baby after death. You may have fears about what your baby looks like, and at the same time, feel uncomfortably morbid in your curiosity. You might feel unsure about whether unwrapping and bathing your baby, taking photographs, or collecting footprints and locks of hair are the right things to do. With support and encouragement, most parents are able to overcome their reservations and realize how much they need and want to do these things.

Because our situation was emergent, we were unable to make any plans prior to Rachael's birth. I shudder now whenever I think about how close I came to not seeing or holding Rachael. At the time, when all I felt was shock, pain, confusion, and emptiness, it seemed impossible for me to see our little girl. Babies aren't supposed to die. It was all so wrong. The pain I felt as I thought about seeing her was almost too much to bear. But grief is so difficult, I can't imagine living with the most terrible regret as well. I felt, and continue to feel, so grateful to my husband, who was going through the same hell and who found the strength to give me no option but to see little Rachael.

—Belinda

We were put into a delivery room, where I would be induced. The nurse asked us questions like, "Will you want to name the baby? Will you want to hold the baby after it's born? Would you like to see the chaplain?" At first we answered no to all three of these questions. We were in total shock. I just wanted to get "it" out of there and go home. I had no idea how attached I already was to our baby.

—Sally

My labor nurse sat on my bed and held my hand. She said that after the baby was born she would take pictures for us. I told her our baby would not look like other babies. She told me that last week she had a baby born with only a brain stem and she was "cute as a button". I knew this woman saw with eyes of love and it reassured me and took away my shame of having a sick baby.

—Leah

Exploring the options

Lavender says that when Oren was born they offered to let me take him home. She says that I said no. . . . Honestly, I don't really remember this, but much of that day was a blur.

—Tanya

When distressed parents are asked questions like, "Do you want to see your baby?" or, "Do you want to take your baby home?" their first impulse is often to say no. It's natural to hastily say no when you are stunned by trauma and grief. And even after saying yes, parents may feel unsure about what to do.

It is hard to know what you want or need during such a devastating time. Without guidance, you may not understand what might be helpful to do and why. You may feel rushed if you're urged to relinquish your baby before you've had sufficient time. You may also feel pressured into making decisions before you can really think them through. Belinda recalls, "We sometimes felt rushed into making decisions... important decisions that we would have to live with forever. We found this very distressing. Making even the most minor decision in a state of shock is very difficult." Alas, a hurried, vague approach by caregivers often leads to regrets for parents.

I remember feeling conflicted. I wanted to hold my son and memorize his appearance and the way he felt in my arms, but I could see that, as time went on and he was handled more and more, his skin became damaged and his color grew mottled. I wanted him to go to the funeral home so that he could look as good as possible for the funeral. Now I wish I could have had time alone with him, time to rock him, sing to him, and to apologize to him for not being able to fight back death.

—Tanya

I called a friend of mine who had experienced a stillbirth just one year prior. I desperately wanted to know two main things from her: what did she do when her child was born still, and did she have any regrets or nightmares from doing these things? The conversation was a very, very short one and filled with many tears and much emotion, of course, and it truly helped me to minimize some regrets that I no doubt would have had today if I had not spoken with her prior to delivering my son.

The main message I came away with after talking to my friend was this: Tell your son you love him... name him... talk to him... hold him... and do whatever the hospital offers you to do with him. So that is exactly what I did. But I didn't know the significance of doing those things she mentioned to me. Why spend time with a dead baby? Why do those memory-making things? Why take pictures? So I was very scared and tense the whole time I was holding Bryce. At times it even felt morbid to be holding my dead baby. I did not know what his body might do. Would it twitch or leak fluids? Would it make noises? Would it smell? The only thing I could bring myself to do with Bryce was to caress his knee, which was the only part of his body sticking out of his blanket.

—Lori

You can benefit enormously when practitioners slow down and gently engage you in ongoing conversations, asking you about your thoughts and feelings on these matters. You get to express your concerns about holding a dead body and hear reassurances that you can hold and bathe and kiss and dress your baby and it can be a beautiful and healing experience. You can hear about specific ideas that other parents have found comforting, meaningful, and memorable. You get to know "*why* spend time with a dead baby" or "*why* take your baby home" when someone explains how this is your opportunity to be a devoted, nurturing parent to your little one.

> *I didn't know how to see the beauty in those final moments. Knowing what I know now, it did not have to be this way. If I'd had a compassionate nurse who was experienced and properly trained in perinatal bereavement care and who could have gently guided me, openly talked to me about fears and how to spend quality time loving and parenting my baby, it could have been a special, cherished, and tender time of getting to know my child's body. And I possibly could have even experienced very meaningful and healing last moments with my son.*
>
> —Lori

When practitioners slow down, another benefit is having unlimited access to your baby. Without arbitrary time constraints, your feelings and wishes can evolve and you get to respond accordingly. You also benefit from practitioners admiring how beautiful and precious your baby is and showing tenderness toward your newborn. Later, as you grieve and every cell in your body is yearning to hold your baby, you can find comfort in the memories of being with your little one and others beholding this beloved child.

Besides informing you, these unhurried conversations can help you adjust to the idea of seeing your baby, take an active role in determining what takes place, and regain some sense of control over the situation. And if you decline to see your baby, you can rest on knowing that you gave this matter the consideration it deserves.

At one point, I asked everyone to clear the room, to let me spend one-on-one time with Bryce alone. I don't know what made me ask for this, but I'm so glad that I did! During this special mom and son time, I told Bryce that I loved him, shed some tears, and told him that I would always love him. I told him that he would always be a part of our family and that I was so sad (or more accurately, crushed to the very depths of my heart and soul) that he couldn't stay with us.
—Lori

I won't ever forget those three days. They helped me acknowledge just how perfect my son was. I had an instinctive need to hold him and look after him and I just had to allow myself to do it. I vaguely remember someone asking if I wanted him put in the morgue. I couldn't even consider it. Part of me, deep down, knew our time was limited. And I wanted every second of it. . . . I spent the night holding Finley, cuddling up to him, sleeping with my baby in my arms. We took photos of the two of us. You can see my tears in them. Even though they're distressing, the memories are precious. I wouldn't be without them. For me, there's nothing more beautiful—more natural—than a mum cradling her baby as he sleeps.
—Mel

Cherished memories

Whatever your decisions about spending time with your baby, you can reflect on all your memories of being with your baby. During your pregnancy, your baby was cradled inside you or your partner. You can remember the kicks and stirrings of a little life. If you held your baby after delivery, you can try to remember how he or she looked and felt. If you delivered more than one baby, having the chance to see all your babies together validates the experience of "my twins" or "my triplets" or more. Although it may never seem like enough, these memories can be cherished evidence that your baby was real and so is your parental devotion.

They wrapped her up and handed her to me. She was such a beautiful baby, and I couldn't believe how much she looked like both of us. She didn't look "babyish" at all—she looked like a little girl. Like a perfect, sleeping little girl. Dan was crying, but I just couldn't stop staring at her. She was so amazing.

—Sally

Oh, how perfectly beautiful she was, with her soft dark hair, her long eyelashes, her long slender limbs. As I held her in my arms, I felt such sadness, yet so much pride. She was surely an angel. We feel so blessed that we were able to hold her, rock her, kiss her and tell her how much we loved her...We named Rachael and we dressed her and cuddled her in her soft "Peter Rabbit" blanket for hours and hours.

—Belinda

We took our time, taking it all in. Looking at all of her body parts. Her hands. Just amazing.

—Anne

My twin daughters were unbelievably perfect and beautiful. They looked like they were sleeping, and I kept expecting them to move or cry. They had dark hair, little rosebud mouths, fat cheeks and tummies, and delicate long fingers. I was surprised how warm their bodies were, but they soon grew cold.

—Darcie

I held Gabriel into the late hours of that night. He was so small but every bit a baby, completely formed. I used my baby finger to form his lips into a tiny circle and I kissed him over and over... I am grateful for the intensity of this kiss, for I can close my eyes and remember the softness of his lips and almost, almost, the smell of his body.

—Mary

Indeed, holding your baby is a bittersweet experience. But it's an important experience, and one that can carry you through your grief. It can also be important for others to meet and perhaps cradle your baby. You benefit from this affirmation and witnessing their expressions of love. Family members in particular can benefit from holding this child who was also a part of their lives and the family tree. This experience can carry them through their grief, too.

My husband held her first and then my mother-in-law and my sister while the nurses tended to me. My mother-in-law sang to her, and my sister held and kissed her. Everyone was saying their hellos and their quiet good-byes.

—Daniela

My friends Alana and Bianca visited. Bianca held Finley, and it meant the world to me. Watching my friends meet my little boy seemed to validate his life, to prove that he was real and that he did exist.

—Mel

My mother and father came to the hospital to meet Bryce. My mother held him, talked to him, and she even requested that the nurse take a picture of her holding him. I was so touched that my mom voiced the desire (and need) to spend time with her grandson. That means the world to me! And it also very much surprises me that she seemed to instinctually know to do these things.

—Lori

Derek, who was twelve, arrived at the hospital unexpectedly with his grandmother after the birth of his brother. He had been afraid to go, but his grandmother had convinced him to come and meet his baby brother and to say good-bye. This was a profoundly important moment for Derek and for our entire family. I think it gave Derek the chance to bond with his brother and to start his own healing and grieving. He has gone on to make several art projects in honor of his brother and to talk to other kids about loss.

—Tanya

Bonding and reassurance

I held her last. I think the sadness really began to set in when I held her. The reality that she was gone began to surface within me. I unraveled the blanket she was wrapped in and looked at her body... She was beautiful. The doctors allowed me to spend as much time as I needed with her and my husband, and we spent the night with her sleeping between us.

—Daniela

Some people may wonder if seeing and holding your baby makes grief more painful because you risk becoming "too attached." But you can remind folks that you've already held your baby in your womb and felt a bond long before your baby died. Others may wonder if it is distressing for parents to see a baby who is dead and possibly deformed.

But imaginings are usually much worse than reality, and as you look through eyes of love, you will be reassured by how normal and beautiful your baby looks. Holding your baby can be a first step toward facing the reality of death and your grief, and facing this reality is what ultimately helps you adjust to it and move toward healing.

I knew he was dead, but I just had to hold him. I had no choice—it was the right thing to do. The only thing to do. Finley's shape fitted into the crook of my arm perfectly. Even now at night I can feel the weight of him there. I remember thinking how lucky I was to be able to sleep with my baby in bed with me. Parents are normally advised against it. So I lay in bed, nursing my baby in my arms, making sure he was wrapped up in his blanket. Sometimes when I moved him, his nose would bleed, and I would wipe it with a wet wipe. The bleeding was a sign that Finley's body was starting to break down, but for me it was a chance to care for my baby.

—Mel

If you are able and encouraged to, spending time with your baby can be remarkably comforting. Seeing your baby's face might reassure you about the peacefulness of death. To hold the body for a while can give you a gentler, more gradual physical separation, especially when you're able to repeatedly pick up and put down your baby over the course of several days. An extended period of time together, whether at home or in the hospital, lets you feel like you've gotten to say hello instead of feeling coerced to promptly say good-bye. And even if you feel squeamish about peeling skin, funny shapes and colors, or escaping bodily fluids, these observations can help you experience the body's lifelessness and the fact that your child's spirit is no longer in there.

The medical examiner wanted to do some cell testing on Adam shortly after he was born. After the testing was over, our delivery nurse asked if we wanted Adam returned to our room. I said no, fearing I could not handle that he would be beginning the process of changing, losing body heat, etc. But my husband asked to see him again. I will always be grateful for his decision. It allowed us more snuggle time. I ended up "rooming in" with Adam until I was discharged the next day. It actually gave me comfort watching Adam go through his changes, especially when I woke up that night remembering I had just had a baby and my body was saying to nurse him. My eyes were able to tell my mind that Adam's soul was gone. The hospital provided us with a wonderful cradle for our use while there. It was such a loving gesture. They treated him very respectfully.

—Leah

I journaled about her body. I wanted to remember every detail about her. I wanted her next to me. We had her tiny body in the baby bassinet. I had my hand on her bed the whole night. I just wanted to have her next to me. To feel connected with her physical being, as long as I could. We did see her body changing, right before our eyes. It was hard. But it was then when I truly realized, she was gone. Her body was turning back to dust. Her soul was with God. I had never seen this before, with a human being, until now. And this was my daughter. My baby. It was life changing.

—Anne

Regrets

I did not explore Bryce's body. I never even thought to do it. No one was there talking to me about why to do this or what other things to consider during this time with him. I so wish that I had a caregiver who could have explained why do these things and who could have helped me to see the preciousness of these final, once-in-a-lifetime parenting moments with my son. Of course, there would still be profound sadness, grief, shock, and confusion in the mix, even with a well-trained, experienced, compassionate caregiver. But I just felt so scared, sad, crushed, and awkward during my time with Bryce . . . and that saddens me to this day.

—Lori

If you were not encouraged or allowed to see your baby, you may feel okay with this—or you may feel quite angry or cheated or desperately curious about your baby's appearance. Even if you did see your baby, it is still normal to have regrets, such as not having more time, not taking enough pictures, not examining every inch of your baby's body, or not doing nurturing things like cuddling, kissing, or dressing your baby. If you gave birth to more than one baby, you may not have been encouraged to hold them simultaneously or take photographs of them together. Many of these ideas may not have occurred to you at the time, or you may have felt uncertain about what was appropriate behavior. Although painful, it is necessary for you to grieve for these missed opportunities.

I think that I felt there was something "ceremonious," something ritualistic about handing her over to the nurse right after the bedside service with the chaplain. Since then there have been times I've wished I'd held her longer, for hours, but I think something in me knew that if I kept holding her as long as I wanted to, that "handing her over" eventually would've been too hard to do. I don't know if I could've done it. They would've had to pry her out of my arms. It was easier to do when I was in shock, partially drugged, exhausted, and had no real understanding of the fact that this was truly the first and last time I'd ever hold my first baby. My beautiful, sweet little innocent baby girl. Such a sweetheart. It's impossible not to cry as I'm writing this.

—*Sally*

If you have any regrets, it may also help to know that you are not alone. Most parents express regret that they were unable to spend more time or do certain things. It can help to look back and remember what an intensely painful, disorienting, and relatively brief time it was. How could you have possibly known or had the wherewithal to do everything that might have been meaningful? Hindsight is 20/20. Even parents who feel like they spent plenty of time with their baby will always wish they could have had more time—a lifetime—with their child.

> *I used to be hard on myself for not doing these things (everything that's on my long list of regrets), but I don't dwell on these regrets any longer. I now accept that I did the best I could under these traumatic, life-changing circumstances and with very little effective guidance from my caregivers.*
>
> —*Lori*

> *I wish I had turned Emily over to look at her back and bottom. But she was so tiny and fragile. I did not want to hurt her, though I never actually thought of doing this, until later, after we laid her body to rest. This is pretty small, though. I kept saying to my husband, "I do not like our circumstances. But I want to have as little regret as possible, with everything." I feel little regret, overall. I feel that God and Emily were guiding us, through everything.*
>
> —*Anne*

Keepsakes

Keepsakes are the objects you can hold on to when you can no longer hold your baby. There are many different kinds of keepsakes you might collect, depending on what is meaningful and comforting to you.

You can gather pregnancy keepsakes such as ultrasound pictures, medical records, maternity clothes, or photographs taken during the pregnancy. You can hold on to keepsakes collected at the hospital, such as locks of hair, footprints and handprints, plaster casts of hands and feet, and the blanket your baby was wrapped in.

> *I have framed Gabriel's footprints, and they take their place on our piano with the boys' pictures.*
>
> —*Mary*

Even the gear you acquired for your baby's homecoming, such as infant clothing, toys, and gifts, can be mementos. If you didn't have the time or opportunity for a baby shower, but you know that particular close friends or relatives had already purchased or started making a gift for your baby, tell them how much you would treasure having these mementos of your baby's short life. They may be uncertain about what to do with the gift and glad to know it would mean so much to you.

You can acquire keepsakes that symbolize your baby and your love, such as plants, flowers, jewelry, dolls, ornaments, beads, fabric, books, stuffed animals, figurines, artwork—anything that speaks to your heart.

You can also create your own keepsakes. Knitting, sewing, weaving, gardening, drawing, painting, engraving, sculpting, building, writing, composing, and designing are just some of the talents you can use to create something to remember your baby by. You can also commission a work of art, perhaps a portrait or symbol of your baby that incorporates a material, context, or visual images that are meaningful to you. These keepsakes can serve to honor your baby's life and provide opportunities to share your baby and experience with others.

If you had a multiple pregnancy and one or more babies died, gathering mementos for each baby can help you to acknowledge their individuality as well as their specialness as twins, triplets, or more. You might collect objects that come in twos or threes or create a portrait that includes them all together. Particularly if you are raising a surviving baby or babies, you may feel it is important to acknowledge each child's membership to a set. Indeed, even though raising a survivor from a multiple pregnancy can present a constant reminder that you should be seeing double or triple or more, your survivor(s) also can be a source of delight and a living tribute to the sibling or siblings who died.

I take comfort in that I will always know what Robert would have looked like, because I can see his face in his lively, healthy twin brother, Cody Alexander.

—*Vicki*

Your keepsakes represent a tangible connection to your baby that you can see, touch, and hold. Keepsakes also connect you to your memories and lend a feeling of being close to your baby or babies.

The photos, prints, and locks of hair are precious to me now. They're all that I have left of them.

—*Darcie*

I have a beautiful bear, and I often find myself hugging it and patting its back. The bear was made just for Rachael, which is so special, as all of our other things were for "a baby."

—*Belinda*

My husband gave me a precious mother and child pendant so I would have something to bring home, as we would not be bringing home a baby . . . . We keep his ashes in our bedroom with his other mementos. It gives us so much peace knowing where his ashes are.

—*Leah*

The hospital gave me a memory box with books, a candle, photos of baby Laure, her blanket, locks of her hair, her footprints, her handprints, and information on support groups in the area. . . . They gave me a blessing certificate with her name on it. At home, we created a "memory shelf" where I keep things from her nursery, photos of her, our maternity photos, cards from her baby shower, pressed flowers from the hospital, her blessing certificate, her urn, and anything that presently reminds me of her. These things bring me comfort. I feel as though she's in the room with us.

—*Daniela*

I still have not been able to wash my bath towel that I used before I delivered Emily. I am not ready to do that. . . . I've followed my heart on many matters. You have to do what feels right for you.

—*Anne*

Photographs

Photographs are particularly cherished keepsakes. They can be made by the parents themselves and by family members, friends, and health care practitioners. Some parents hire a professional photographer, while others tap into the network of photographers who volunteer their services for grieving parents. (See Resources in the back of this book.)

> *We have some beautiful photos from my best friend, who is a photographer and artist, and from another photographer [with the company] Now I Lay Me Down to Sleep.*
>
> —*Tanya*

For parents, the most meaningful photographs tend to be those that show their nurturing and devotion to their baby. Your most treasured images might be of you holding your baby, gazing at your baby, or bathing and dressing your baby. You might also appreciate the photos that show others cuddling and admiring your infant. It's natural for you to especially cherish photographs of your baby's unclothed body, your baby's hands, feet, and face, and even what makes your baby unique, such as birth defects or anomalies. Black-and-white photographs can be particularly beautiful, as they put the focus on relationship and emotion and soften the often distracting colors of clothing, decor, and skin tones.

Later, as you grieve, these photographs provide concrete evidence that your baby was real, not just in your dreams. You can study these images and remember the details of what your baby looked like. You can see how you spent your time with your newborn and feel affirmed as your baby's loving parent. If you had twins or more, photographs of your babies together is one way to acknowledge their special relationship. Photos can also jog hazy memories blurred by shock, trauma, birthing pains, medications, and sleep deprivation. Even if you never look at them, you know you have them, and they link you to the baby you miss so much.

> *Oren is my first-born. I am glad that I have pictures of him so I know that he was real. I get to have a photo of my son just like other proud moms, even if I rarely choose to show it to anyone.*
> *—Tanya*

If you decline the opportunity to take photos and later wish you had some, ask your hospital staff whether they made and saved some for you. With new privacy and patient autonomy laws, policies are changing on this, but in the past hospitals routinely provided this service, since parents without photographs of their stillborn babies may regret that decision later. Some parents, particularly those who regret not having photographs or are dissatisfied with the ones they have, hire a portrait artist to draw a likeness combining their memories and a composite of family baby pictures.

Bereavement rituals

Bereavement rituals are activities that honor your baby, memorialize your baby's life, and express your devotion. Ritual can be particularly comforting to the bereaved when a death is sudden, unexpected, or traumatic, and stillbirth certainly qualifies. Common rituals for babies include naming, baptism, bathing and dressing, burial or cremation, funeral and memorial services, and recognizing significant days such as due dates and birth dates in meaningful ways. Traditional rituals making a comeback in the United States include taking the baby home—where parents provide after-death care and perhaps hold a wake or funeral—and green burial.

Any time you engage in a ritual that pays tribute to your baby, you are expressing in heartfelt ways your identity as a parent to this child. Ritual can be an important part of your healing.

> *Ritual is very important to me, having lost both of my biological children—the one miscarried and then Oren. I am still a parent even though my children have died. I have a strong need to parent them. Some of this need can be fulfilled by coparenting Derek, but how does one parent a dead child? . . . It may sound odd, but by participating in honoring your child, you are parenting him or her.*
> —*Tanya*

Rituals can be ceremonious or subtle, public or private, elaborate or simple, traditional or created by you. They can occur immediately after your baby's death or down the road, whenever you feel ready and able. Rituals can also be ongoing, such as tending a garden, wearing a special piece of jewelry, or donating to a charity. Rituals can be recurring, such as lighting a candle, visiting the grave, or buying flowers on special days. Ritual can be commemorative, such as creating a plaque, gravestone, or memorial fund.

While rituals can be painfully sad, they can also give comfort as they help you acknowledge your baby's life and death and validate your grief. Rituals can also invite others to witness and share your grief and offer comfort. Do what feels right for you.

We had our wedding florist do Emily's funeral flowers. And she used
all of the flowers from my wedding bouquet. It was very special
having her and those flowers. We plan on doing a tree out back in
remembrance of her. Maybe a pink dogwood.

—Anne

Unfortunately, in many religious and legal traditions, stillborn
babies fall into a gray zone when it comes to ritual. For example,
certain ceremonies are considered inappropriate, and state governments do not bestow a certificate of birth. These traditions are based
on the fact that stillborn babies are not alive after birth, but this lack
of recognition is often distressing for parents. How can it be denied
that this baby lived, that this baby was born? Not being officially
baptized or named seems unnecessarily cruel. Not getting a birth
certificate can feel so hurtful and insulting, and only adds to your
trauma.

Some clergy are flexible and will do tailor-made blessings for
stillborn babies. Ask the hospital chaplain or your own clergy for
help. Unfortunately, state and federal governments are uncompro-
mising, but some hospitals recognize this oversight and offer their
own "certificate of life." There are also bereaved parents' organiza-
tions that offer certificates especially for stillborn babies (see Resources in the back of this book).

We had Emily baptized two days before, when she was in my tum-
my. We had our priest come to the hospital after she was born, and
he did it again. We just wanted to be sure that we did "everything"
for her. Baptism is for the living, but we still wanted it.

—Anne

Naming

You may wonder if naming your baby is appropriate. Giving your baby a name is a way to acknowledge your baby's existence and individuality. It is personal and lasting. Your baby deserves to be named. You may use a name you had in mind all along, or you may settle on your baby's pet name bestowed during the pregnancy or choose a special name after you discover this baby is dying or has died.

Whether the name is formal or an endearing nickname, given before birth or long after, it will give you an easy way to refer to this child and include him or her as a member of your family.

Bathing and dressing your baby

A baby's first bath is a cherished milestone that you might want to experience. Even if you are confined to bed, your nurse can put a waterproof cover over your lap and give you a water basin and supplies. You may want to immerse your baby in water, or you can give your baby a sponge bath. You may want to gently apply baby lotion or scented oils to your baby's body, hands, and feet.

Ask for advice on what will maintain the integrity of your baby's skin. If you'd prefer that your nurse bathe your baby, you can ask that it be done on you or next to you, so you can feel included.

Examining your baby's entire body is another way to get to know your baby. You may feel shy about doing so, but this attentive inspection is a natural expression of your devotion and reinforces your identity as a nurturing parent. You may notice features you recognize in other family members. Tenderly handling your baby's body begets special moments that become cherished memories and affirm your parenthood.

I was looking forward to bathing her. Because we didn't have a baby bath, the nurses allowed me to undress her and pretend I was bathing her. My husband took video footage of her "bath." This was the most meaningful and special moment for me.

—Daniela

You may have also gathered cute newborn clothing that you were looking forward to using. Mel notes, "We dressed Finley in all the different outfits—a kind of fashion show—and took photos of him wearing them." Or you may prefer the ease of simply swaddling your baby in blankets. Some parents want to keep their baby unclothed, as nature intended, and feel their infant's skin against theirs. If you wish, you can carry out all these options.

In total we were able to spend three days in hospital with Finley. I will be forever thankful for this. . . . I had decided that I wanted my last memory of Finley to be bathing him, dressing him, and reading him a story before leaving him in that cozy room with a midwife, so he would not be alone. We now have special videos of these moments. They are the most extraordinary and moving videos I have ever seen. A mum caring for her baby, changing his nappy, washing him, and getting the poppers done up all wrong. Then cuddling him as she reads him a bedtime story, wraps him in a blanket, and lays him in his cot to sleep. It looks like the most natural thing in the world.

—Mel

Bringing baby home

Back before hospitals and funeral homes were commonplace, death and the care of dead bodies happened in the home. Especially for a newborn, providing after-death care at home is simple and straight-forward. Germs are not an issue, as the baby carries only what was in the womb. Chemical embalming is an option but rarely required by law, since keeping the body cool can be just as effective in slowing deterioration. Parents can layer dry ice (replenished daily) among blankets in a basket where the body can be kept when it's not being held and warmed in loving arms. If your baby is tiny, keeping the body in a sturdy container in your refrigerator works well, too.

> We took our Emily home with us, until her funeral. I just wanted her with us. Home with us...
>
> I remember taking a moment before we placed Emily on my lap. I was in the wheelchair. This is how we carried all of our babies out of the hospital, on my lap. Sadly, my baby was in a container, in a pink diaper bag. I thought, What would people think of this, if they knew? Not that I would care. But how sad would they feel for all of us? This poor couple giving birth and taking their dead baby home.
>
> I asked the funeral director what they would do with our baby, if we handed our baby over to them. He said, "We would put your baby in our refrigerator. That is what we do with the bodies to preserve them." I said, "We have a refrigerator. We can put our baby in there. So, our baby can be home with us." I remember putting Emily in there and saying, "I am so sorry that I have to put you in here. But this is where it is best for your body." I would kiss her container every night, and say, "Good night. I love you."

—Anne

The tradition of home care has persisted in Ireland, Australia, New Zealand, and many other parts of the world. Because home care holds much value to bereaved parents, this tradition is making a comeback in some countries.

If you can take your baby home or if you have a home birth, you get to immerse yourself in your parenting role and experience a tiny morsel of normalcy—leaving the hospital with your baby in your arms, sleeping with your baby, greeting loving visitors, and showing your baby around the house and neighborhood. Elizabeth recalls when Mike, the funeral director, first invited her to visit Thor in the funeral parlor, and then nonchalantly suggested that she take him home.

> *I gaped at him. I had thought I would never see Thor again when we'd left the hospital. I was almost as grateful as if Mike had told us he could bring Thor back to life . . .*
>
> *No one bothers to tell grieving families their options. Unless you discover the home funeral movement, which we didn't. Unless Mike is your funeral director, which he was.*
>
> *"Shoot, take him home if you want!" Mike said. "Take him overnight, spend some time with him. Maybe you have some friends who'd like to visit with him? It'll be fine, just keep him in a room that's cool."*
>
> *Our bedroom, I thought, my head spinning. We always turn down the heat there during the day, to save energy. And at night the whole house is cool anyway. But of course that wasn't the point. Our bedroom was where Thor was supposed to have slept with us, where I was supposed to have nursed him. Where we were supposed to have said hello.*

This was when I understood: Thor was our baby. He did not belong to the hospital. He did not belong to the funeral home. He was ours.

—Elizabeth

Funeral homes

Whether you bring your baby home or not, you can get assistance from a local funeral home. Many establishments offer free or discounted services to families of infants. If calling around to inquire is too much for you to bear, ask a friend or family member to test the waters. You'll want to find an establishment with people who are compassionate and sensitive to your unique needs and desires, particularly with regard to your wanting to spend additional time with your baby and how you want the body treated.

An accommodating funeral home can easily transport your baby or help you with any necessary permits to provide your own transportation, whether you want to bring your baby home or deliver the body to the funeral home yourself. If you prefer, they can keep your baby for you, still making him or her readily available to you until burial or cremation. If you don't want your baby's body embalmed, they should be able to refrigerate it for you or advise you on keeping the body cool in your home. They can also guide you in selecting a casket or urn, finding a burial plot, exploring green burial (see the next section), and planning the funeral or memorial service. If you decide on green burial, they can point you toward green cemeteries in your area or beyond.

Burial and cremation

You may find it difficult to choose between burial and cremation, as neither is a comforting thought. In fact, you may be outraged at the whole concept. You don't want ashes or a grave—you want a baby!

What is the perfect time to bury Thor? I thought, the space above my eyes curdling. The perfect time is no time. We can't bury him. We just got him.

—Elizabeth

If you decide to bury your baby, a green burial may be the most comforting option. An alternative to chemical embalming, impermeable caskets, and concrete vaults, green burial involves the simple concept of keeping the body cool until the family is ready to wrap it in a shroud or place it in a container of natural fibers and offer it to the earth, the way burial has been through the ages. Green burial can seem like the kindest, gentlest alternative and the most natural process. You may sense that it's the most protective and nurturing choice you can make for your little one.

Right after we were told there was no heartbeat, I told my partner, Lavender, that I wanted the baby buried in a green cemetery. I didn't want him filled with chemicals and put in a concrete box. Lavender called a friend to start finding out where there were green cemeteries. The friend found one forty-five minutes away and called us back. She told Lavender that we would need to provide a basket in which to bury the baby.

Our son rests in a beautiful handmade basket (made by a dad who lost his son), wearing a sweater that my mother had made for me when I was a baby. . . . Oren is buried in a little grove of trees at a nature preserve. It is about as lovely as lovely can be. Someday I hope I can be laid to rest nearby.

—*Tanya*

Green burial or not, you can make or choose a unique burial container that speaks to you as a person and a parent. And by filling it with symbolic and important objects, you can feel like a part of you is accompanying your little one.

Even as we drove to the cemetery, I wanted our baby with us. So Emily rode on my lap. She was in a beautiful urn/casket that my husband and I picked out together. We did not cremate her, but the only containers available for her, because she was so small, were ones for cremations. We put pictures in her container, items from the mass, the boys drew more pictures for her, my husband and I wrote letters to Emily. So did our moms. We put special blankets in her container and vault. My baby blanket. Something green, too. The flowers from her casket. Her baptism cross. A rosary from the Vatican, blessed by Pope Benedict. We wanted her container and all that was in there to be special and thoughtful.

—*Anne*

If you decide on cremation, you can make a nurturing gesture by enclosing keepsakes that stay with the body and become part of the cremains.

We cremated her body and held a quiet funeral service. I asked that our maternity photos, photos of my husband and I, as well as a flower decoration from her nursery be burnt with her body. The crematorium allowed it. This made me feel like we were indirectly with her as she was being cremated. She was not alone and will never be alone.

—*Daniela*

Whether you bury your baby's body, scatter the ashes, or keep the ashes in your home, you may find it comforting to know where the remains are. Their location can give you a place to go when you want to feel close to your baby.

Most distressing was the knowledge that I was physically separated from Gabriel until I picked up his ashes. Gabriel's ashes rest in a red velvet lined wooden box with a wolf carved on the outside, a gift from my sister. They remain in our bedroom until Brian or I die. Part of me wants to place him with my father's ashes, but I can't part with them, and my dad will surely understand.

—*Mary*

On Earth Day, we planted Robert's ashes beneath a new tree at our church's outdoor chapel. That tree will forever be "Robert's tree," and we can enjoy its shade each summer Sunday as we worship in the fresh air. For us, it was a fitting ending to such an emotionally draining experience.

—*Vicki*

If you have regrets, acknowledge your sorrow about this and then figure out ways that you can memorialize your baby in a special place. Planting a tree, mounting a plaque, or erecting a bench or statue can give you a meaningful place to go where you can reflect on your baby and directly acknowledge that precious life.

Funeral and memorial services

I never, ever thought we would have to think about such things. It's just not fair. Right now we should be tired and excited and holding our baby in our arms. We should be up to our armpits in nappies, not thinking about hymns and flowers and readings.

—Mel

We displayed the little gown that Adam wore, a couple pictures, a twelve-inch tape measure, a certificate of birth with tiny little foot-prints . . . and the hospital wristbands that were never used. There it was, life to death in three 20 x 30" frames.

—Fred

Planning a funeral or memorial service is another shocking set of decisions to make. But this ritual can gather loved ones around you at a time of great sorrow. It is also another way to honor your baby. A graveside ceremony can be particularly tender and meaning-ful, as this is a profound parting.

There were poems and prayers, songs and drumming. Our son was buried in a lovely handmade basket wearing all sorts of special clothing that was made and chosen for him. Oren means "pine" in

Hebrew, and when he was placed in his grave he was covered with pine boughs and flowers. We, his mothers, put in a few strands of our hair, and I poured in the colostrum that I had pumped since the birth. It was strange that a day that was so sad could also be extraordinarily beautiful.

—Tanya

I wish we'd had a special memorial service for Bryce and invited all of our family and friends to come support us and see his picture displayed. I think a memorial service could have also allowed family and friends to truly see this was our child who died, and not just some tragic event that happened to us at a hospital.

—Lori

A funeral gives people a chance to pay their respects prior to burial or cremation. A memorial service is appropriate any time you feel ready or decide it's something you want to do. You can arrange for a formal service and invite many people, or you can keep it small and informal. You can also do it by yourself, alone. Do whatever feels comfortable and comforting to you.

If it feels too overwhelming to plan a service, or if you simply want additional commemoration, you may consider attending a memorial service sponsored by a local hospital or a bereaved parents organization. You can also join in bereavement charity fund-raisers, such as a "walk to remember," in honor of your little one.

Around Christmastime, I went to the Compassionate Friends candle-lighting service here, and my parents and brother went to one in another state. Not only do you get to speak your child's name and

*light a candle in remembrance, but you also get a chance to meet
other bereaved families.*

—Tanya

When it comes to bereavement rituals, it is normal to wonder
what you might have done differently and how it might have eased
the pain. Remember, your decisions regarding rituals are based on
your circumstances, mindset, needs, and options offered at the time.
And it is never too late to memorialize your baby in ways that are
meaningful to you.

*One thing I've appreciated more than anything is the way my
parents continue to remember and memorialize Helen. It means
so much to me not to feel like I'm solely responsible for making sure
that people don't forget about her. My parents had a bench put in
a park in the town they live in, with Helen's name and birthday
carved in it. It makes me feel good that they have a place where
they can remember Helen, and other people can see her name, too.*

—Sally

7

Grieving

When your baby is born, the silence is deafening; you will always remember the stillness. And what should have been one of the best days of your life has become one of the worst.

In the months to come, you may have many moments when you doubt that you can survive this ordeal. Your longing, anger, sadness, and despair can run so deep that you wonder if you will ever emerge from this abyss called grief. You may worry that your devastation will wipe out your ability to cope. Healing seems impossible when mere survival is in question.

I'd had some difficult times in my life in the past, but there was nothing I could compare to this grief. I could've never fathomed that it was possible to feel this bad. There were days that I thought I would physically die from sadness and emptiness. It was so scary. And now I think it was really normal, and healthy, too. But I started to wonder if there was any way I'd ever smile or laugh again.
—Sally

In this chapter, you will find brief and basic information about grieving, along with suggestions for coping. While gaining insight into grief and coping cannot shield you from anguish, it can prepare you for what lies ahead and reduce your distress by giving you guidance and helping you set realistic expectations.

Accept your need to grieve

Because grief is so distressing to endure, many people believe that grieving is something bad, and it's to be avoided or gotten over as quickly as possible. But it isn't a problem to be solved—it's a process that unfolds over time. As you move through your emotions, you gradually let go of what might have been and adjust to what *is*. Grief is what enables you to come to terms with your baby's death.

> *I've come to accept that grief is very hard work. It's very individual and personal, and no one can tell you how to grieve. There is no pattern to grief. I just feel what I feel.*
>
> —*Belinda*

> *The tears have stopped now, but the pain lingers on. Because I'm a man, society has decreed that I should put this matter behind me and get on with the business of life. In trying to do just that, I denied myself the due process of grieving, which, in hindsight, more than likely did more harm than good. If I could turn back the hands of time, I would allow myself to open up and realize it's all right to be scared and feel totally out of control. . . . Never again will I be a victim of the silent crying.*
>
> —*Ron*

Certainly, there will be times when you hold in your grief. A flood of tears may not be appropriate or comfortable at certain times or in certain places or with certain people. But you can save it for later, rather than burying it forever.

Even during your darkest days, by grieving you are also moving toward healing. It is your grief that will take you to the other side.

I did know that I would eventually feel better and still be able to remember Helen and integrate her life and death into our lives. But there were plenty of times I wished someone could just knock me out and wake me up when I was going to feel like some version of me again. Then I came to realize that living through it and "working" on it, and being brave enough to face it and let myself feel the depths of the sadness, that is what eventually made it livable. And I did it . . . and I'm still doing it . . . and I think I'll always be doing it. I'm really proud of myself.

—Sally

View grief as a complex process

Grieving parents experience a wide range of pronounced and bewildering emotions, including numbness, disorientation, yearning, guilt, failure, anger, and despair. You may experience physical symptoms such as aching arms, tight chest, poor appetite, and fatigue. You may struggle with body image, sexuality, and self-esteem. You might have hallucinations of hearing a baby cry. You'll probably feel preoccupied with your baby and feel so scattered and disorganized and isolated, you might wonder if you are going crazy. It's even normal to feel you just don't have the will to go on. These are all parts of grief. However, if you make plans to commit suicide, SEEK HELP. This qualifies as a MEDICAL EMERGENCY. Do not allow crippling grief to kill you. Suicidal plans are a hallmark of serious depression, and you can benefit from medical treatment.

While you certainly expect to feel sad after your baby's still-birth, you may not be prepared for the storm of physical sensations and agonizing emotions.

I was really surprised at the physical effects of grief. For me the most dramatic was the effect upon my eating. I found it so hard to eat. In the early weeks, a good day was one where I had eaten once and managed to dress.

—Mel

There was this crazy dichotomy between my body being this beautiful sacred space that was the only home my son had even known, and horror at the fact that I had carried death inside of me. The body stuff has been hard.

—Tanya

I remember about three months after we lost Helen, I got up in the morning to get ready for work and felt crummy as usual. Most days I just felt like I was a zombie, and I just did everything mechanically. I ate my cereal, which tasted like cardboard; I got in my car, which seemed to drive itself to my destination. But that morning, I was feeling especially out of control. It was so tiring and scary to feel so sad and empty all the time. I remember crying hysterically and yelling "HELP!" over and over to the empty house. I just didn't feel like I could keep going.

—Sally

Little things, like never knowing the color of their eyes, haunt me still.

—Darcie

Grief is not something you can experience in a neat progression of stages or finite set of emotions. There are no universal timetables. And there is no right or wrong way to grieve. Your grief will be as unique and complex as you are.

Hold realistic expectations for your grief

Grieving is a fluid experience in which your painful emotions will ebb and flow. Grief is unpredictable, too. It is often impossible to foretell how you will feel from day to day, or hour to hour, or month to month. And grief is not a steady climb, but rather like a roller coaster, with ups and downs. The downturns can be discouraging, but remember that they are normal, and as time passes they will become fewer and less distressing. Just knowing that grief is fluid and unpredictable can make your journey easier.

> *The first couple weeks were weird; I realize now that I was still in some form of shock. I would break down crying for a while, and then I'd just stop and feel "fine." I remember those first two weeks when I woke up in the morning I didn't instantly feel bad, and I remember thinking, "This might not be as hard as I would've thought." Wrong. It was right around the two-week mark that I stopped the cycle between either crying or feeling "fine," and I started to just have this heavy, horrible, hopeless feeling that stayed—and it stayed for a long time.*
>
> —Sally

Some of the downturns are somewhat predictable. As your initial shock wears off, you will probably feel worse for a while. You may also have "anniversary reactions." At first, you may feel most unsettled or sad at certain times of the day or week. As time passes, you may notice that you feel especially blue at certain times of the month or year. It's as if your body remembers and associates certain conditions with your baby's life and death. But just as the downturns do, these anniversary reactions will lessen in frequency and intensity over time.

> The baby only rolled over at 11 PM and 3 AM. I used to wait up till 11 PM and wake up at 3 AM because I didn't want to miss this active time. After Adam died, I cried at 11 PM and woke up at 3 AM to a motionless, empty womb and cried some more.
>
> —Leah

> I struggled most during the night. The worse parts were the nightmares and flashbacks. I found out that Oren died in the evening. Most days it seemed like my grief would start to overwhelm me after dinner and push on through until the wee hours of morning. As time passes, and with therapy, the evenings and nights are getting easier.
>
> —Tanya

Grieving is hard work and takes a lot of energy. Whatever you are feeling, it's normal, it's common, and it's okay. You're entitled. It is also normal to seek professional help. If you think you would benefit from counseling, get it. You are worth it.

> There were times in the months following Helen's death when I'd start to feel better and then be surprised when I plunged down

into a deeper grief than I'd ever felt before. . . . I heard a therapist speak, and she said, "There's no such thing as going backward; it's impossible to go backward. If you feel like you're going backward, it just means you really stepped into the middle of something big, and you've reached another stage of acceptance." I really liked that! And it's so true. If you never have those bad days, then you really aren't making any progress at all—you're just existing, and not really living.

—Sally

Accept that you and your partner will grieve differently

Because everyone's grief is unique, you and your partner will surely walk different paths. Your paths may frequently intersect, but you will experience different emotions, ups and downs, triggers, and timing. What's significant or helpful to you might well be insignificant or unhelpful to your partner, and that's okay. Refrain from interpreting the other's silence as "not caring," or the other's intense grief as "never getting over it." Remember that the best support you can provide is a listening ear, resisting the urge to "fix it," and reassuring each other of your devotion to your relationship. Indeed, many couples emerge stronger than ever as this crisis bonds them more tightly and spurs them to improve communication skills.

I thought that my husband, Chris, was trying to be "strong" for me, us. About a month after we had buried Emily, I felt alone because he had accepted that Emily had died and was with God. And the "whys" he did not ponder as I did. But we try to be open and honest in our communication and try not to judge or criticize. I knew that my husband loved and still does love our baby. Our daughter. And he was and is sad that she died. And that is all that matters.

—Anne

Identify the feelings you experience

Identifying your emotions can help you perceive grief as more manageable rather than a confused, knotted bundle of pain. The following is a summary of some of the common emotional states that parents experience.

Shock and numbness: You don't feel much of anything because you simply cannot absorb the fact of your baby's death.

Next morning I woke up, and all the drugs had finally worn off. That was when the first stage of reality hit. I just felt dead inside. I sat in the hospital bed and looked out the window. The sun was out, but everything seemed to have a gray tinge to it, like somebody had dimmed the lights on the whole world. Little did I realize that was probably the best I was going to feel in a long time.

—Sally

Denial: You harbor fantasies that your baby is still alive somewhere, that you can recover your baby somehow, or that soon you will awaken from this nightmare.

I remember my mom calling my husband, saying, "We're at the hospital, and you need to come... You just need to come here... They can't find the baby's heartbeat." Oh, God. She'd actually said that. This couldn't be happening. It was so surreal. It was like a horrible dream.

—Sally

Disoriented and overwhelmed: As you come to grips with your baby's death and struggle to comprehend all that has happened, you feel bewildered and overcome with grief.

In the beginning, the emotional pain was just completely unbearable . . . I felt so very alone, confused, and lost!

—Lori

I had my first daughter, Mia, at 11:42 that night. . . . Her sister, Grace, came at 11:53. Their births were unbelievably easy physically, although emotionally devastating beyond belief. My husband and I sobbed as I delivered our beautiful baby girls. Such a sick and backward negative of the joy we had expected and felt at our first son's birth. The only thing that kept me from screaming and screaming was the knowledge that our parents were right outside the door. They were already so frayed that I thought they would go crazy if I did.

—Darcie

Anger: You are mad, frustrated, impatient, irritable—because your baby's death is so very unfair and infuriating. Anger also comes from the helplessness you feel because your baby died and there was nothing you could do about it.

I was so mad with God, too, even though I knew in my heart that He wasn't responsible. I just wanted Him to explain to me why drug addicts and child abusers are allowed to keep their children.

—Belinda

I remember not wanting to think about God at all—if there is a God, how could He take Finley away from us?

—Mel

Guilt and failure: You feel somehow responsible for your baby's death. (For more on this, see the next section, "Question your sense of responsibility for what happened.")

What did I do to cause this? I still have not found a reason as to why Emily died. I look at her ultrasound pictures, and she looks perfect. I just do not get it.

—Anne

There must be a way to banish the nightmares; to quiet the inner voices of judgment and guilt; to ask "what now?" instead of "why?" or "why me?" There must be a way to look at myself in the mirror and smile.

—Tanya

Sadness and despair: You feel devastated, distraught, empty, hopeless, hurt.

Nothing I can do or say will bring her back. No matter how many tears I cry, it will not change that Emily is not here with us

physically. That is hard to accept. I know that her soul is alive in
Heaven. But it is still hard.

—Anne

Each week it gets a bit easier, although I still cry almost daily
and have strong and ugly feelings that I hope will fade. I can't yet
envision the future; it seems so bleak and empty. The past is also
so painful when I remember all the hope and joy I felt. Sometimes
the sight of a pregnant woman will fill me with tears, not out of
jealousy but sadness for my former innocent and proud-bellied self.

—Darcie

Naming your emotions increases self-awareness and productive reflection. For example, when you're feeling numb, you needn't
think of yourself as uncaring or unfeeling, but rather in shock.
When you're feeling irritable, you can see it as part of grief rather
than holding others responsible for your ire. And when you find
yourself in a negative loop of self-blame, you can seek out reassurance that you are not at fault. Being aware of your feelings and state
of mind allows you to thoughtfully respond to the world around
you rather than react or lash out in ways you might later regret.
You needn't analyze or justify or rush through your feelings. Simply
observe and let them flow through you.

I have a good understanding that feelings, although intense, cannot
actually hurt you, and that avoiding them actually makes it worse.
I have learnt how to sit with painful feelings and know that they
are just that—that they are a memory or a reaction to a memory,
and that the event is not happening now. I found that often if I

looked at the feeling and allowed it instead of suppressing it, it went very quickly.

—Mel

Question your sense of responsibility for what happened

A sense of responsibility arises from the belief that you should have been able to protect your baby. Even if you know rationally that you were not at fault, it is human nature to draw conclusions about cause and effect. You may find yourself grasping at straws in an effort to make sense of how this could have happened.

Although the doctors have told me numerous times that there was nothing I could have done to save her and that umbilical cord accidents are no fault of the mother, I struggle with feeling a sense of responsibility. If I had slept differently or been more alert to her movements or had not laid on my back that time, she would be alive.

—Daniela

During my pregnancy, on the night of my Blessingway, I was overcome by the beauty that I had witnessed and by the love and excitement of so many toward the little person inside me. Later I wondered if he died because I had too much happiness.

—Tanya

For some parents, feelings of responsibility are expressed as a sense of failure. You may feel like you've been an incompetent parent or feel inadequate as a man or a woman. It's normal for the mother to feel betrayed by her body, and her sense of failure can run deep, injuring her body image, self-confidence, and desire for sexual intimacy.

Autopsy and chromosomal analysis revealed Gabriel was a very healthy baby boy, and I am thankful. I so hope that he didn't suffer any pain before or during his death. I am afraid to discuss my feelings of responsibility. I made healthy choices throughout my pregnancy but can believe no other explanation for his death than my body's failing him.

—Mary

I guess I had been "hoping" that the doctor would have been able to tell me that Bryce died due to something being wrong with him. It really, really upset me to know that he was healthy, full-term, normally developed and just days away from being born . . . but then he died anyways (because my body somehow failed him). That was very hard to get over.

—Lori

Feelings of responsibility are also expressed through a sense of guilt. Mothers especially struggle with guilt. You may wonder how you could be so helpless to prevent your baby's death. If the cause of death cannot be determined, you may fill in the blank with your imagination and hold yourself accountable. If you experienced complications during the pregnancy, you may be particularly wracked with guilt.

When there are no answers, guilt and blame can be overwhelming... Perhaps a day went by when I forgot to tell her how much I loved her—that's why it happened. I shouldn't have had that quarter glass of wine—that must've caused it. Or perhaps it happened because I was so sure she was a boy that she must have felt unwanted. Oh, and then there was the idea that I was bound to get a terrible, fatal disease and God took her first before leaving her here without her mother.

—Belinda

Guilt is a natural emotion. To cope, recognize that no one has total command over their reproductive anatomy or childbearing fortunes. Remind yourself that what happened was beyond your control and not your intention. Understand that there is a difference between *feeling* guilty and *being* guilty, between *feeling* a sense of failure and *being* a failure.

After Oren's death I felt like I had somehow caused it since I have worked with birth (midwifery) and death (hospice). My partner, bless her, says that she thinks my soul knew this was coming and I have been doing this work for years to prepare myself to get through this with my own son—though I did not know it. Whether or not this is true, it removed a huge amount of guilt from my shoulders. And my midwife said I couldn't have done anything to Oren because I'm not that powerful.

—Tanya

If you faced agonizing decisions, it may help you to remember that you were in the impossible position of having to choose between *terrible* and *horrible*. Whatever your decisions, they were right for your particular circumstances and the information at hand. Most importantly, they arose out of your love for your baby.

My husband and I do not feel responsible for his disease. We had no idea that this disease even existed before we had Adam. I do have feelings of responsibility toward ending the pregnancy. Adam was dying in utero. He had a zero percent chance for survival. Via ultrasound, it looked like a horrible way to die. By beginning the labor, it seemed the best way to ease his suffering—hastening his death.

—*Leah*

Your feelings of responsibility will fade as you fully grasp the fact that you had neither the power nor the plan to harm your little one.

Embrace your vulnerability

As you question your sense of responsibility and shed your feelings of guilt or failure, you will realize you are truly unable to always avoid tragedy. This can be a scary, unsettling feeling, but embracing your vulnerability allows you to focus on the present rather than worry about controlling the future.

We feel frightened now—open to all the random tragedies in the universe. Our sense of control, fairness, and trust changed forever... I guess we're trying to learn to live more in the moment, since now is all we can really ever count on.

—*Darcie*

Embracing your vulnerability also helps you adopt a "wondering attitude," which is the opposite of being controlling and attached to a certain outcome. When you're attached to an outcome, you think, *I wish... I hope...*, and when things don't go according to your plan or timetable, you're in suspense, impatient, struggling, distressed, disappointed, or devastated. In contrast, when you adopt a wondering attitude, you think, *I wonder. I wonder how this will turn out. I wonder what's in store for me. I wonder what the plan is.* You remain curious about how your life will unfold. You stop trying to exert control over everything that happens, and you don't feel burdened by misplaced guilt. You do your best, but you distinguish between what you can control and what you can't. You know when to simply go with the flow, thereby eliminating the suffering caused by fruitlessly trying to swim upstream.

This wondering attitude is considered spiritually centered by many faith traditions. It doesn't erase your need to grieve, nor does it discourage you from your dreams, visions, and search for excellence. But rather than struggling to bend the universe to your will, you trust that what happens is for your highest good—even when you can't see the river for the waterfalls.

Accept your preoccupation with your baby as a natural part of grief

Early on after having endured a stillbirth, thinking about your baby is constant and inevitable. You may feel totally preoccupied and filled with longing and yearning. You may think you hear your baby cry; you may wake up at night and wonder for a second why your belly is so small. You may think about returning to the hospital and searching for your baby. You may be able to feel the sensation of your baby kicking inside you. Your arms may ache to hold your little one. You may dream vividly about your baby. If you're a mother, your recovering body adds to your distress; leaking fluids remind you that there *should* be a baby. Your longing may seem so unbearable, you don't know if you can go on.

Consumed by grief, you may feel so scattered and distracted that it's all you can do to get to the grocery store, stare at the bananas, and then leave without getting a thing. You may avoid the baby food aisle for months. You may question how everyone else can keep going when your world has come to a screeching halt. As Sally recalls, "I felt so out of control. I just thought about Helen all the time, and everything else seemed so pointless and trivial." It may seem as if everything triggers thoughts of your baby.

> *Little things remind me of Adam's death. Exiting any parking ramp, I remember leaving the hospital, handing the attendant my parking ticket stamped OB. He asked, "What'd you get?" Or driving by any funeral home, I will never forget making the initial call to make cremation arrangements. A very dignified gentleman said, "Yes, we can help Adam with his situation." I thought, "His situation? No, he's our son, and he's much too young to have his own situation."*
>
> —Fred

Your preoccupation is a sign that your mind (and body) is processing—and sometimes fighting—the traumatic reality of your baby's stillbirth. Even though your bond has been altered by death, you still have powerful biological urges to nurture and protect your baby. As a mother, the biochemical postpartum changes in your body put you in parental overdrive. You may feel like you should be able to recover this baby, if only you could figure out how. You may be obsessed with your baby's body, wanting to be with it, to know where it is, to keep it warm. Your obsession can lead to hallucinations and mothering behaviors that make you question your sanity. But you are not insane. You are missing the very thing that would give meaning to these natural feelings and behaviors: your baby.

> *Since Oren's death, it has been rare for me to sleep through the whole night. I think part of this must be physiological wiring that prepared me to be up at all hours with the baby.*
>
> *—Tanya*

As time goes on, your urges and intense longing will fade. For now, accept yourself where you are. The resilience of your mothering urges is evidence of your biological inheritance as well as the depth of your maternal love. And although a supremely painful reminder that your baby is gone, your milky breasts also offer affirmation. *There was a baby, and you will always be his or her mother.*

Dwelling on your baby can also benefit you by making you feel close to your baby, which can ease your trauma and make your good-bye feel more gradual. There are many things you can do to feel the comfort of your baby's presence. You might decorate your baby's grave, wear a special piece of jewelry, caress your keepsakes, write a letter to your baby, look at photographs, and review your cherished memories. Smell and sleep with your baby's blanket, cuddle a stuffed animal or baby doll, cradle pillows in your empty arms, lie down on your baby's grave, or talk to your baby's ashes. When you feel the urge, do what makes you feel close to your baby.

Pursue what helps you cope

There are many activities and resources that can help you grieve and thereby heal.

- Set aside time for yourself and your grief. Let your feelings flow. You may discover that whenever you release a flood of feelings, you will be brought into a meditative, peaceful calm.
- Let yourself fall apart. Falling apart is scary, but each time you crumble you can pick up the pieces and put them together in a new way. Most parents can look back and see that each new way is a better way, and that this cumulative transformation is healing.
- Respect your own needs. As you grieve, be gentle with yourself. Remember that you deserve to get what you need. Determine what you can do to feel better and move forward.
- Try alternative therapies. To release or ease painful emotions, try acupuncture, aromatherapy, art therapy, therapeutic massage, and other forms of therapy such as Reiki, Rolfing, myofascial release, and movement therapy.
- Attend to your physical health. Adequate rest, nutrition, and physical activity are keys to boosting energy and positive brain chemistry. Try nutritious juices and shakes when your appetite is off or you aren't motivated to prepare food. Moving your body can improve your outlook and help you sleep better.
- Structure your day. This can help you feel more oriented and productive. Mel reports, "The first thing I did was to make a timetable. I literally programmed my day—times to eat, what to eat, times to drink water, time to dress, time to wash, time to go for a walk, time to read. I ticked off what I

had done each day. This helped to add structure to the long days and nights."

- Abide with nature. A vast body of research confirms that direct contact with nature increases mental health and psychological and spiritual development. Benefits include stress reduction, improved self-confidence, and a sense of purpose, meaning, and belonging. You can find solace in gardening, walking, hiking, bird-watching, or any other activity that gets you outdoors. Even sitting in a sunny window with a view of greenery or the company of indoor plants can be soothing.

- Practice meditation. Meditation quiets the mind and reduces distress, giving you respite from the chaos of grief and bereavement.

- Practice mindfulness and reframing. For example, if you are ruminating on the thought, *My baby died because I must've done something wrong*, mindfulness and reframing means being aware of, questioning, and casting aside this distorted perception and embracing this compassionate reality instead: *My baby died of natural causes, and I had no power to protect my baby from this fate.*

- Wrap yourself in memories of your baby. Memories are an important resource that help you process your experiences, move through your grief, and fold your baby into your life story.

- Talk about your baby. Telling your story to friends, relatives, or anyone who will supportively listen can be therapeutic, helping you garner support, process what you've been through, gather insights, and boost self-awareness.

- Write about your baby. Keep a journal of your memories, experiences, ideas, and feelings. Even if you don't consider yourself "a writer," unloading your thoughts onto paper can relieve you of the burden of holding them inside. In the process, you're also creating a keepsake.

- Write a letter to your baby. This direct communication is another way to process this emotional time, express any regrets, seek forgiveness, let yourself off the hook, or demonstrate your love. Then, if you wish, imagine or write your baby's reply.
- Attend a support group. There is therapeutic value in meeting and talking with other parents who truly understand what you're going through.
- See a counselor or therapist. This extra support can fill in the gaps. He or she can acknowledge and validate your feelings and assist you in seeking coping strategies and effective ways of relating to others.
- Accept the support of others, however clumsy it may be. Tell people what you need. If they are true friends, they'll be glad to know.
- Write letters to whomever you wish to vent—the rude neighbor, the kindly stranger, your doctor, the hospital, God, Mother Nature, fate. Don't send them; this writing is for you.
- Seek information. Find books, articles, and websites about coping with grief, medical or spiritual issues, or whatever you're looking to understand or master.
- Read blogs and other personal accounts of infant death, grief, and bereavement. Seeing how others have prevailed can inspire your own resilience.
- Be open to advice that seems helpful and pass by whatever isn't.
- Engage in creative, musical, or athletic endeavors. These encourage the expression of emotions or release of tension

while making you feel like you can accomplish something constructive.

- Lean on the parts of your spiritual beliefs or religious faith that comfort you.
- Ask for guidance or reassurance from other parents who've been there.
- Find respite in those activities, people, and moments you can enjoy.
- Try to recognize anything positive—discovered strengths, new growth, enlightened perspectives, meaningful pursuits, better relationships. Although it can be a struggle to find treasure in adversity, doing so can help you heal and honor your child's memory. In time, you will feel ready to do this.
- Make a conscious decision to survive. After a while, you can decide whether to remember your baby and move forward with what you've gained, or remain stuck with what you've lost. Many parents mention that eventually they reach a point where they just decide to stop wishing it hadn't happened and start learning to live with it. When you are ready, you can do that, too.
- Remember that your grief is normal, and you are not alone.

Have faith that eventually you will feel better

In spite of the unpredictable ups and downs, you can expect your grief to slowly soften over a period of several years. This may seem like an interminable length of time, but as the months pass, the ups do become more frequent and longer lasting. Eventually you will discover that you can remember your baby without falling apart.

Your sadness and longing won't disappear entirely, but they will mellow as you adjust and adapt. Some people call this "resolution of grief" or "moving forward" or "getting on with life," but this does not mean that you leave your baby behind. Your baby's death may never feel acceptable, but you can accept that it happened, adjust to the unexpected change in your relationship with this child, and realize that you can simultaneously remember and move through this experience, gradually integrating it into the big picture of your life.

I have had only one dream about Gabriel. He was about ten months old, beautiful dark brown hair, dark brown eyes, porcelain skin with glowing red cheeks. He wore a black and white checked pair of overalls. He was crawling away from me, toward darkness. He turned around to see me, sat up on his knees, and smiled. I felt peace in this dream, and I hang on to his smile until the day I will certainly see it again.

—*Mary*

In trying to make sense of your life again, you can find meaning or extract something positive from this ordeal. You can see the positive aspects of having this baby come into your life, including how you've changed and grown as a person. You can also acquire a sense of peace. You'll never forget this baby, your life will never be the same, and you'll always bear scars, but your broken heart can heal. Embracing personal growth and living your life to its fullest is perhaps your baby's most powerful legacy.

For now, I will take the baby steps that my son never got to take. I will wake up each morning and say, "I love you," to those living and dead whose strands of life are so intertwined with mine. I'll eat good food and drink water. I'll cry when I need to cry, and try not to judge myself as I grieve in my own fashion. I'll exercise my body and be grateful for its strength and resilience. I'll look at the sunlight in the trees and sit in Oren's beautiful garden. I will discover that I can laugh and dream again. And I will strive to push through my vulnerability and fear to tell our story to the world. Oren is silent; he needs me to be his voice.

—Tanya

Resources

From the folks at Fulcrum Publishing

Dear Parents,

We are so sorry that your baby has died. We hope that this small book offers you support and comfort. If you found this book helpful, we highly recommend *Empty Cradle, Broken Heart: Surviving the Death of Your Baby*, also by Deborah L. Davis, Ph.D. In that classic book, you will find additional support and information on grieving, coping, healing, and subsequent pregnancy, as well as comfort and reassurance in the quotes of other parents who've been there. Please know that you are in our thoughts.

For additional support, information, and resources, please visit the author's websites and professional blog:
- www.NICUparenting.org
- http://nicuparenting.org/Bereavement.html
- www.perinatalhospice.org
- www.psychologytoday.com/blog/laugh-cry-live

If you wish to donate books to bereaved parents or buy books for a program that serves them, we offer you a bulk discount. Call 1-800-992-2908.

Permissions

Elizabeth (Heineman) is the author of *Ghostbelly* (Feminist Press, 2014), a memoir of deep maternal love, bonding, and grief. She is quoted from her essay "Still Life with Baby," winner of the 33rd New Millennium Writings Award, nonfiction category, http://new-millenniumwritings.com/showdb.8.php?w=88.

Nicola (Daly) is quoted from her book Sasha's *Legacy: A Guide to Funerals for Babies* (Steele Roberts Publishers, 2005).

Mel (Scott) is quoted in part from her memoir, *After Finley*, which is available through her website, www.finleysfootprints.com.

Tanya (Mudrick) is quoted in part from her essay "Reconstructing Self."

Lori (Martini) is quoted in part from her personal account, which appears on her website, www.HealingFromTheStart.com.

Information and support

Vital Statistics

Fetal and Perinatal Mortality, United States, 2006. Volume 60, Number 8 August 28, 2012
http://www.cdc.gov/nchs/data/nvsr/nvsr60/nvsr60_08.pdf

Stillbirth Information, Research, and Advocacy

International Stillbirth Alliance, www.stillbirthalliance.org

Wisconsin Stillbirth Service Program (WiSSP),
www2.marshfieldclinic.org/wissp/

Bereavement Photography

Todd Hochberg is a pioneering bereavement photographer
based in Chicago. His website holds beautiful images and
articles about the history and value of photographs for parents,
www.toddhochberg.com.

Now I Lay Me Down to Sleep, a network of volunteer photographers, www.nowilaymedowntosleep.org

Bringing Your Baby Home

www.bringyourbabyhome.com

Donating Breast Milk

The Human Milk Banking Association of North America
(HMBANA), https://www.hmbana.org

A bereaved mother's personal account of donating breast milk,
"A Donor Mom's Story from Mothers' Milk Bank of Ohio,"
January 2006 newsletter of the Human Milk Banking
Association of North America,
https://www.hmbana.org/downloads/2006Jan_newsletter.pdf

Bereaved Parents Support Groups

The premier network of support groups across North America is Share Pregnancy and Infant Loss Support, www.nationalshare.org.

Multiple Birth

Our Newsletter, The Center for Loss in Multiple Birth (CLIMB), www.climb-support.org

Books and Keepsakes

A Place to Remember, www.aplacetoremember.com
Centering, www.centering.org

Perinatal Bereavement Care

Bereavement Training in Perinatal Death, manual and programs by Resolve Through Sharing (Bereavement Services), www.bereavementservices.org

Professional support, networking, position statements, and practice guidelines, the Pregnancy Loss and Infant Death Alliance, www.plida.org

Links to position statements, practice guidelines, recommendations, and best ideas in bereavement care, for professionals and parent advocates, http://nicuparenting.org/Bereavement_Care.html

CuddleCot, an easy-to-use system that keeps baby's body cool for parents, http://flexmort.com/cuddle-cots/

About the Author

Deborah L. Davis, PhD is a developmental psychologist who writes books that support parents through crisis, including the death of a baby (*Empty Cradle, Broken Heart; Stillbirth Yet Still Born*), premature birth (*Parenting Your Premature Baby and Child*), parenting in the NICU (*Intensive Parenting*), making decisions about end-of-life care (*Loving and Letting Go* and *When Courage Lies in Letting Go*), and perinatal hospice (*A Gift of Time*). Over the past 20 years, parents have found comfort, hope, and healing in her books. She has also written professional articles, position statements, and book chapters on medical ethics, perinatal bereavement care, and NICU parenting, and she advocates for training and supporting the health care practitioners who work with these families.

Dr. Davis is forever inspired by the resilience parents demonstrate and the transformation that takes place after surviving trauma. She also writes a blog for Psychology Today online. Dr. Davis lives in Denver, Colorado.